EVANGELICALS ON THE CANTERBURY TRAIL

Morehouse Publishing
PO Box 1321
Harrisburg, PA 17105

Morehouse Publishing is a division of the Morehouse Group.

Unless otherwise indicated, Scripture quotations are from the Revised Standard Version of the Bible, copyrighted 1946, 1952, © 1971, 1973 by the Division of Christian Education of the National Council of the Churches of Christ in the USA, and are used by permission.

Library of Congress Cataloging-in-Publication Data

Webber, Robert.
    Evangelicals on the Canterbury Trail: why evangelicals are attracted to the liturgical church/Robert E. Webber.
        p. cm.
    Reprint. Originally published: Waco, TX: Word Books, 1985.

    ISBN 0-8192-1476-0

    1. Evangelicalism and liturgical churches. 2. Converts Anglican.
3. Episcopal Church—Membership. 4. Anglican Communion—Membership.
I. Title.
[BR1640.W42   1989]   88-30406
270.8'2—dc19   CIP

Cover design by Rick Snizik

Cover photos by Jason Smith

Printed in the United States of America

EVANGELICALS
on the Canterbury Trail

Why Evangelicals Are Attracted to the Liturgical Church

ROBERT E. WEBBER

MOREHOUSE PUBLISHING
HARRISBURG, PENNSYLVANIA

Contents

Preface

Recently, when I was giving lectures at an evangelical college, a faculty member asked if we could meet somewhere privately.

When we were seated in the privacy of his office, I could tell by his darting eyes and fidgety mannerisms that he was nervous. Clearing his throat and adjusting his body to a comfortable position, he began. "The reason I wanted to talk with you is that I find myself following a spiritual journey similar to yours. My family and I have been active members of a local evangelical church for a number of years, but find we need something more. We now attend the early service at a local Episcopal church, then go to the church where we are members for Sunday school and morning service. That's okay for now, but we can't go on forever like that. Can you give us some advice?"

Then there is another scenario that happens in my office quite frequently. A student will drop by and say, "Can I talk to you about the liturgical church?" While some are interested in becoming involved in the church, others are only curious.

There are other students who are already involved in liturgical churches. They want to talk about the concern expressed by parents who don't know how to deal with the fact that their child is being drawn to a Christian tradition other than their own.

And when I speak in liturgical churches, there is always a great deal of curiosity about evangelicals. Who are they? How do they differ from fundamentalists? What kind of influence might they have in the liturgical church?

These four groups of people—those who are in a serious spiritual pilgrimage into the liturgical tradition; students and others who may be curious; parents who are bewildered; and liturgical Christians who want clarification about the evangelicals in their midst—are the people to whom this book is written.

Evangelicals on the Canterbury Trail will not answer every question. But it will at least provide an introduction to the phenomenon of evangelicals moving toward the liturgical tradition. While I cannot provide any statistics stating how many people are involved in this movement, I can say that I am overwhelmed by the number of people I meet who are either journeying the pilgrimage described in this book, or at least somewhat influenced by the concern to restore aspects of historic Christianity inadequately represented in their own church.

A book like this cannot be written without the help and influence of many people—friends, teachers, ministers, students, and colleagues. I wish to express special thanks to deaconess Leanne Payne, Father George Monroe, Father James Barr, and Bishop James Montgomery for their help and availability to me during my entrance into the Episcopal church. A word of appreciation also goes out to the Wheaton College administration and to my colleagues for allowing me to journey into the liturgical experience without accusing me of having abandoned the evangelical tradition. And to the contributors to this book whose names appear with their stories, I give thanks. Finally, I wish to acknowledge the expertise and dedication of my editors Floyd Thatcher and Kathleen Mohr. Because they too have traveled the path to Canterbury, their sensitivity to the subject has gone beyond duty into personal involvement and commitment.

Introduction

No, I don't object to evangelicals going into the Episcopal church. As a good Baptist I believe in the Liberty of Conscience. I would also say that the Kingdom of God is broader than any denomination. One of my daughters is an Episcopalian. How do I feel about it? The answer is that it's her business, not mine.

Harold Lindsell
Editor Emeritus
Christianity Today

For most people Reformation Day, October 31, 1972, was just another day. But for me it was a special day, a turning point in my life. About 10:30 that morning I was sitting on a large blue chair in Edman Chapel between the president and the chaplain of Wheaton College, waiting to speak to a crowd of more than two thousand Wheaton students and faculty.

I always get nervous when I speak, and today was no exception. I could feel my hands moisten, my throat go dry, and my stomach tighten as I watched students running, squirming, and twisting while attempting to find their seats.

Many of these students' faces were familiar to me—close friends or students from my classes. Others I didn't recognize. Nevertheless, I felt I knew something about all their happy faces. We were united by a common background. For many of us, family structures, family expectations, and church experiences were similar. It didn't matter whether we came from Maine or California, Minnesota or Florida, the cultural context of our evangelical experiences was as familiar as an old shoe.

I wondered, "What will they think of my sermon today?" But I didn't have much time to think about it because we were called to sing Luther's well-known hymn, "A Mighty Fortress Is Our God." The organ was up and out full tremolo and the students bellowed out the hymn with great enthusiasm. I watched those faces as we sang. I knew that many of these students were from leading evangelical homes—children of evangelical pastors, college and seminary professors, college presidents, missionaries, leaders of mission agencies, directors of magazine and book publishers, and worldwide leaders.

The hymn ended.

The president prayed the invocation.

I was introduced.

"Today," the president explained, "Bob Webber, a member of the Bible and Religion faculty, is going to speak to us on the glories of the Reformation. The sixteenth century was a great period in church history, and we wait with anticipation to hear of God's good work in that era, a work from which we still benefit today."

"Oh, oh," I said to myself, "that was the wrong thing to say for this speech. The president isn't going to like what I'm going to say."

I stood to my feet, walked with some uncertainty to the pulpit, and began. "The modern historian Jaraslov Pelikan has written of the 'tragic necessity' of the Reformation. As Protestants we have frequently heard talks on the necessity of the Reformation. My guess is, however, that most of us have never heard a talk on the tragedy of the Reformation. On this Reformation Day I wish to speak to you on that forbidden subject—'The Tragedy of the Reformation.' "

The next Sunday I walked into an Episcopal church to stay.

Why would I, the son of a Baptist minister, become an Episcopalian? Why would I, a graduate of Bob Jones University, walk the Canterbury Trail? Why would I, an ordained minister of the Reformed Presbyterian denomination, forsake my orders? Why would I, a professor at a main-line evangelical college, risk misunderstanding and put my career in possible jeopardy to follow my heart?

Why is it that my journey is not an isolated example, but an illustration of a much wider phenomenon within the evangelical community? What is it about the liturgical church that has attracted so many of us through its doors? What conditions within Evangelicalism may have created the desire for this journey into a more ancient tradition?

The answers to these questions are not easy. Yet, they must be addressed because a growing number of people are moving out of fundamental and evangelical church groups and into main-line churches. I want to write to those whose hearts are pulling them in this direction and to those who are puzzled or upset over this movement.

Specifically, this book is about my personal journey and that of a number of other people into the Episcopal church. But the current immigration is not exclusively into that church. Many evangelicals are returning to Presbyterian, Lutheran, Methodist, and other historic denominations as well. Thus, this book is about the movement back into the main-line church in general.

I am well aware that you may have one of several reactions to our pilgrimages. For example, those of you who find your faith within a more recent tradition may have some questions about what you read here. Please keep in mind that I'm not asking you to join us on the same journey. But I'm urging you to try to understand and empathize with those of us who are on the Canterbury Trail. Others of you may find that some of the longings and deep-found desires that have moved us toward Canterbury are needs that you seek to fulfill in your own Christian experience. Even though you may not be headed toward Anglicanism, you may identify with us and try to incorporate some of its practices into your own tradition.

Frankly, I think there is much from the Anglican tradition that can enrich and strengthen the evangelical church. But Christianity is like a diamond. To see it in all of its fullness and beauty, we must see it from all of its sides. Anglicanism has a side to it that is not found within the evangelical church. And the opposite of this is true. Evangelicalism has strengths that can enrich and strengthen the Anglican tradition as well.

So, if you are an Anglican reading this book and thinking, "Aha, finally these evangelicals are seeing the light," please don't become too smug just yet. Or if you are an Anglican saying, "Yipes, an invasion of evangelicals in our midst, who needs that? Not me," I ask you to suspend judgment as you read. You might be pleasantly surprised by our contributions to your church.

Since the Sunday that I entered the Episcopal church, I have often reflected on my pilgrimage in faith. I have thought not only about the years preceding that Sunday, but the more than a decade that has passed by since then. To help me better understand and describe my journey, I think of it in terms of walking through three stages of faith: familial faith, searching faith, and owned faith.

Familial Faith

The first seven years of my life were spent in the deep heart of Africa, in the jungles of what was then called Belgian Congo. My parents, who were missionaries in the small village Mitulu, were committed fundamentalists. Both my mother and father had traveled independently to Africa where they met, married, and worked together to evangelize the natives. My father even took safaris into the jungle to reach the pygmies who had never seen a white person, let alone heard about Christ. Sometimes I would go with him.

There were three of us kids—me, an older sister, and a younger brother. When my brother became seriously ill, my parents decided to return to America, where my father became pastor of the Montgomeryville Baptist Church in Montgomeryville, Pennsylvania, a small town about twenty-five miles west of Philadelphia.

The parsonage adjacent to the church was home, and I was the *preacher's kid*—a constricting label I couldn't escape. I was the kid who couldn't go to the movies, the kid who had to keep Sunday as a holy day (no sports), the kid who had to watch everything I did and said.

But I wasn't just a preacher's kid. I was also a fundamentalist Baptist. From an early age, it was thoroughly ingrained within me that I was both a fundamentalist *and* a Baptist. Being Christian wasn't enough. The best Christians were fundamentalists. And the best fundamentalists were Baptists. Catholics were pagan. Episcopalianism was a social club. Lutherans had departed from the faith. Presbyterians were formalistic. And Pentecostals were off-center. Now I may not have been taught these overly simplistic convictions explicitly. But I must have picked them up somewhere in my youth, because for a long time this is what I believed with all my heart. I'll call this type of belief system *familial faith.*

Searching Faith

I tell my students at Wheaton College that the college years are good years to test familial faith. I ask, "Do you believe what you believe because your parents believe it, or do you believe what you believe because you have looked at the options and you own it?" There is a certain amount of risk to *searching faith,* that transition period when you test your familial faith in order to come into *owned faith.*

During my years as an undergraduate, I was not invited to enter into searching faith. On the contrary, searching faith was taboo. To ask genuine questions, to test the options, to be open to other traditions was seen as a sign of doubt.

For example, I remember a number of times when the college founder, speaking in the chapel, would cup his right hand over his mouth, jerk the upper part of his body backward, look to the ceiling, and cry, "So you want to know where a man stands with God?"

Now everyone wants to know where a man stands with God, so this question always grabbed the attention of the student body. "You only have to ask him one question," he said, replying to his own challenge.

Of course, we sat there with our attention fixed on this dynamic man. "What is that question?" we thought.

Then came the answer, thundering through the auditorium, "What do you think of this university?"

This kind of attitude does not foster intellectual curiosity. Instead, it encourages the perpetuation of a fixed faith through memorization and an institutionalization of thought. But then, we all have a tendency to institutionalize our particular brand of the Christian faith and treat our interpretation of the faith as truth.

At any rate it was this inflexible spirit that I encountered in college that first sent me into searching faith. I said to myself, "This can't be the one and only interpretation of the faith. How can we cancel out all the godly people of church history and the many other living traditions in which people express their faith? Could it be," I asked, "that God has a mold into which he wants to stamp us all?" Because I couldn't come to that conclusion, I found myself wandering away from that particular fold, leaning toward a more inclusive rather than exclusive view of the faith.

I continued to encounter an exclusivism in faith in the seminaries I attended. It gradually dawned on me that *everybody* holds not only to the faith, but to an interpretation of the faith. As I studied historical theology in graduate school my eyes became opened to numerous boxes into which God and the faith had been placed. And, as the result of the long-range impact of an ecumenical fellowship that I joined and about which I will tell you later, I gradually became aware that behind all of these various interpretations of the faith is one faith.

Owned Faith

I often tell my students that the history of the Christian faith can be compared to an artichoke. The kernel is found in the very center, hidden by layers of leaves. The layers represent the traditions we have built around the truth, traditions that sometimes stand in the way of encountering the truth in its naked power.

Just as we need to peel off the leaves of an artichoke to get to its heart, so in the Christian faith we need to peel away the layers of tradition that take us to the heart of faith.

My own experience is similar to this. I have come to appreciate all the traditions for what they are. They are not the truth, they are the interpretations, the layers of secondary truth which we have added to the common core of the faith that comes from the apostles and the primitive church.

The church that I now claim as my own and the one that is owned by the other contributors to this book is a particular tradition, the Anglican tradition. But I think we would all say that Anglicanism itself is not the truth, it is one way of describing and living out the truth of Jesus Christ, living, dying, and rising again for the salvation of the world.

The actual substance of faith, the content that stands behind every Christian tradition, is Jesus Christ. It is the Jesus interpreted by the apostles and summarized in the Apostles' Creed. This is the Christ I believed in as a boy, the one whom I searched to know in a deeper way in all the educational institutions I attended, the one whom I now worship in the liturgical church.

So, my pilgrimage into the Anglican tradition is no repudiation of orthodoxy. Rather, it is the affirmation of six aspects of orthodoxy that were not adequately fulfilled for me in my Christian experience. I'll simply state those reasons here and reserve comment on them until the next section of this book.

For me, Anglicanism preserves in its worship and sacraments the sense of mystery that rationalistic Christianity of either the liberal or evangelical sort seems to deny. I found myself longing for an experience of worship that went beyond either emotionalism or intellectualism. I believe I've found that for myself in the Anglican tradition. I also felt a need for visible and tangible symbols that I could touch, feel, and experience with my senses. This need is met in the reality of Christ presented to me through the sacraments. These three needs—mystery, worship, and sacraments—are closely related.

At times I also felt like an ecclesiastical orphan looking for spiritual parents and a spiritual identity. I am now discovering my spiritual identity with all God's people throughout history, by embracing the church universal and a holistic perspective on spirituality. These three needs—historic identity, an ecclesiastical home, and a holistic spirituality—are also closely related.

In the first section of *Evangelicals on the Canterbury Trail,* I describe my own spiritual journey in these six areas of faith. I'm not sure that one has to become an Anglican to satisfy these longings that I and others like myself have experienced. I know many Christians in other traditions who also experience the inclusive reality of which I write. However, all of us whose stories are included in this book feel the Anglican church is a refuge, a home, a place where an intuitive and inclusive Christianity is taught and practiced.

In the second section, six evangelicals who, like me, have made the trek into the Episcopal church will tell their stories. All of these persons, except one, are presently employed in evangelical institutions. I deliberately chose these people who have remained evangelicals because I feel their experiences say something very positive about evangelicalism. For me, evangelicalism is certainly a lot less exclusive than it used to be. It is rapidly developing an inclusive spirit—a spirit in which all Christians who own the core of faith, no matter what their tradition, are acceptable.

Another matter of interest is that the presence of an increasing number of Anglicans in the evangelical movement and evangelicals in the Anglican church may cause ripples of influence to move in both directions. What will the increasing number of Anglican theologians and leaders within evangelical institutions mean for the evangelical church? And what will the presence of evangelicals in local Episcopal churches, seminaries, and various agencies mean for the Episcopal church? Surely these movements contribute to the breaking down of the walls that have separated us in the past. As you read the stories of these six contributors, mutually penetrating influences will become more apparent.

I hope no one will construe this book as an attack against fundamentalism and evangelicalism. I have high regard for my conservative past, and I know many devout Christian people who find great joy and spiritual fulfillment in this tradition. It is not my intention to deny the validity of their experience.

As I write, I recall an experience I had recently. I was visiting my parents in Mechanicsburg, Pennsylvania. On Sunday night we went to the Independent Baptist Church of Shiremenstown, the church my parents regularly attend.

I watched people file into the church and attempted to catch the spirit of what was happening. The organ was playing favorite evangelical music, such as "Wonderful Grace of Jesus" and other similar upbeat testimonial songs.

As the people took their seats and greeted one another with a handshake, a hug, or a kiss, I felt a tremendous sense of joy among these people of God. A man sitting down the row from me was tapping his foot to the music and keeping time with his gum-chewing mouth and bouncing head. His frequent repetition of "Amen" and "Praise the Lord" made it obvious that he was worshiping.

I would never think of suggesting that these people become Anglican. Nor do I for one moment think my Anglican expression of the faith is a higher form of spirituality. Yet, it is a fact that many people like me, who have been reared in a fundamentalist or evangelical background, have made a journey into the Episcopal church or another more main-line tradition.

This book explores the question "Why?" without making unnecessary negative judgments. It attempts to describe the larger phenomenon of crossing over into what may seem to many fundamentalists and evangelicals to be "foreign territory."

I hope you will read *Evangelicals on the Canterbury Trail* with an open mind and an understanding heart.

Why the
Anglican Tradition?

1.

A Return to Mystery

The first time I entered an Episcopal church I felt like I had stepped into a medieval atmosphere. Wonder and awe. I don't mean medieval in the bad sense. I mean it in terms of simply being in the presence of God. The experience of mystery keeps drawing me back again and again.

Gary Madison
Graduate Student
Wheaton College

Earlier I mentioned that I grew up in Central Africa in a little village called Mitulu. The village was actually a small clearing in the middle of the thick and nearly impenetrable forest for which Africa is so well known.

I still have many fond memories of that forest. I remember the huge trees that soared upward into the sky, weaving their branches into each other like fingers. Hanging from the trees were long, thick vines that made great swings in my more sporting moments. Beneath them were thick, deep green brush and seven-foot-tall elephant grass. Sparkling brooks ran through the forest, occasionally interrupted by a tumbling waterfall. And the forest's silence was broken only by the cries of the monkeys, the sounds of many birds, the rushing winds, and gurgling waters. But most of all, I remember the sense of fear that hovered over it all. All who stepped into the jungle were aware of the stalking lions, the man-eating leopards, the crocodiles, and poisonous snakes. Yet I was enchanted by its mystery. I felt then, as I do now, the overwhelming power of God's natural creation. There is a feeling of something beyond—a deep and impenetrable mystery that beckons one to enter into its reality by simply experiencing its power.

For the first seven years of my life I lived in the jungle and knew nothing about Western civilization except what I was told. I had never seen a big city until my family stopped in Shanghai on our way home to America. I was amazed at the huge, tall buildings of that concrete city, the masses of people, the quickly moving taxi cabs, the clatter of the restaurants, and my first sighting of a trolley car. For some reason, however, industrial and technological society has never given me the same feeling of awe and wonder I experienced in the forest. There seems to be something explainable about what man has accomplished in God's creation, while the creation itself remains a mystery.

As I grew up in the Western culture of America and began attending school, the mystery of my childhood was soon replaced by the Western ideal of the explainable. Everything, even religious experience, I learned, was to be subjected to reason, logic, and observation. Claims to mystery, to wonder, and to the experience of things too deep to explain were looked upon as primitive, anti-intellectual, and weak-minded.

Rationalistic Christianity

This concern for a rational understanding of the universe spilled over into my religious education, particularly in college and seminary. For example, I still remember my first survey course of the Old Testament. The teacher walked into class carrying a large syllabus that included more than one hundred pages of facts. In his introduction he told us that all we needed to know for his course was in the syllabus. Memorize it! Indeed, the syllabus represented a masterpiece of organized information about the Old Testament. It contained the important names, dates, and events not only in general, but specifically for every book and chapter of the Old Testament. What happened on the third day of Creation? Who was Moses' mother? What was the name of the last judge? How many feet long was Solomon's Temple? How many chapters are there in the book of Psalms? What were the names of the people who helped Nehemiah rebuild the walls of Jerusalem?

I found myself conscientiously making lists and memorizing names, dates, events, and a whole host of seemingly irrelevant data. By the time the course ended, I had memorized a thousand or more facts. But if someone had asked me, "What is the message of the Old Testament?" Or, "What kind of sensitivity do you now have to Jahweh; to his love, compassion, and election of Israel; to his relationship to the world and to the peoples of the world; to his concern for justice in the land for the poor and the oppressed?" I would have looked at this person with a blank stare. I didn't learn anything about the message of the Old Testament, about the movement of God in history, nor did I learn how to discern his contemporary presence and power in the world for me and for the peoples of the world. For me, the Bible had become a textbook of facts to be memorized and regurgitated on an irrelevant test.

Much of my seminary education was characterized by the same mentality. Here the concern was not so much for facts but for proof of Christian convictions. For example, I remember a study of the resurrection in a course on apologetics. The emphasis of this study centered around the arguments—the "answers"—to be offered to those who deny the resurrection. I have no objection to the critical examination of the New Testament resurrection accounts, nor do I object to a critical evaluation of the arguments set forth against the idea of the bodily resurrection of Jesus Christ from the grave. What I do object to is the treatment of the resurrection or other issues of doctrine that turns matters of faith into scientific issues. I found that the scholastic attempt to prove the resurrection as a scientific fact did not increase my faith at all. If anything, it took away the mystery and the power of the resurrection and turned it into a dry fact that had little to do with my personal struggle to live a Christian life. While I could repeat all the reasons why it was important to believe in the resurrection, I could no longer speak of the meaning of the resurrection in my own life. What was once a mystery that empowered my life was now an objective argument tucked away on a shelf in my brain.

I didn't know it at the time, but I was being swept away into evangelical rationalism, into a proof-texting Christianity, into a Christianity based on scientific inquiry. Christianity was no longer a power to be experienced but a system to be defended. I had left the impenetrable forest and entered the technological city.

My study of the Bible now turned into a defense of its inspired authorship. I remember in particular a course I took on the Pentateuch. I recall my eager anticipation as I entered that course of study. I really wanted to learn more about the message of the first five books of the Old Testament. I knew how important they were to the Jewish faith, how foundational they were to the Jewish and later the Christian view of God, who entered into covenant with his people to redeem them and to form them into his special people. I wanted to be exposed to the works of God for Israel, to come closer to the one who revealed himself as a redeeming and caring God to these people he called out of Egypt. But how disappointed I was in that course! It seemed the teacher's purpose was to defend the Mosaic authorship of these books. Rather than challenge us to experience the power and mystery of the God who began to work in history, he presented us with arguments against those who denied that Moses wrote these books. I still can't read the Old Testament without being upset over the time I wasted in that class reducing the mystery of God as revealed in the Pentateuch to an exercise in intellectual gymnastics.

I experienced the same frustration in my courses on systematic theology. The assumption of these courses was that the Bible is a propositional revelation of God to the world. It is, as some evangelicals say, the mind of God written. Since God's mind is written in a book, we who have been made in the image of God (especially gifted with a mind) may study God's mind written and reach a fairly comprehensive, but not exhaustive understanding of him. We are the meat-eaters—the ones who are to grow in faith and knowledge of God through our intellectualization of Christian doctrine.

But the opposite happened to me. I felt as though I was following after the God on the blackboard, the God in the textbook. My experience was simply this: the more certain I became about my ability to defend God's existence and explain his character, the less real he seemed to me. But I was afraid to admit my feelings to anyone else, and I scarcely acknowledged what was happening in my soul. I was drying up spiritually. The reservoir of God's presence in my life was running low. But forget that. It really didn't matter. I had the answers. And, after all, I had been taught that the answers were what made the difference.

Giving Up Rational Christianity

In 1968 I came to Wheaton College fresh from my doctoral studies. I was full of knowledge, armed with the answers, and anxious to help the students of the late sixties who were feeling the desperation of the Viet Nam war, the loss of meaning to life, and the despair of that historical time.

One of the first courses I was asked to teach was a class called Christian Doctrine. Here's my chance, I thought, to give them the goods, to show them how rationally defensible the Christian faith is and how reasonable it is to believe in the Christian system of things.

I had heard an evangelical leader say, "I believe in Christianity because it is the most rational explanation of the universe. Show me another system more rational and I'll embrace that and give up my Christian faith." Of course, that person always went on to say that he had studied all the religious and philosophies of the world, and that he believed there wasn't any view more rational than the Christian faith. So he was always on safe ground when he uttered his challenge. I also thought I could rationally defend the Scripture as God's mind written and then proceed to systematize the truth of Scripture into my reformed box.

To be honest, I loved the box into which I had placed God. Everything fit together so neatly and nicely. First, I derived a great deal of security from my system. I didn't have an answer to all questions. But I had *the* answer. If a student asked why there was evil in the world, or why the God of the Old Testament seemed to ordain wars, or did the Bible teach double predestination, all I had to do was punch my theological computer and out came *the* answer. It gave me a feeling of power, a sense that I was always on the side of the angels. I had developed a smug complacency about my ability to handle the mysteries of life with a touch of knowledge.

Second, wrapping God up in my neat little system gave me the power of judgment. I remember when I first started to teach, a local Arminian challenged me to a duel in the classroom. I took to this challenge as one would take to a sport. Great fun, I thought to myself. We met in my classroom and debated the five points of Calvinism. I was certain I had nailed him to the wall with my clear logic and impressive assembly of biblical texts. I was elated, almost jubilant over what I considered to be my victory. My system, I thought, was simply superior to that of anyone else. I could quickly put the Catholics, the dispensationalists, and the charismatics in their place, because I really believed their understanding of the biblical data and use of logic was faulty and dangerous. Any "true" Christian with a knowledge of the Bible and common sense would agree with me. I was convinced of that. Reason alone would eventually force all into conformity with my interpretation.

I think I already felt that my reliance on reason and the attitude it created was pretentious, even outrageous. But, at the time, it was all I really knew. It had been modeled for me by many of my teachers. It was a position held by many evangelical leaders. So who was I to question its validity?

However, early indications of doubt did begin to emerge in my first year of teaching at Wheaton College. I really wanted to reach the students that were turning away from the faith at that critical moment in time. As I talked to them about their faith and attempted to "keep them in the faith," so to speak, I became gradually but increasingly aware that the answers didn't work. They simply weren't buying into my system. Actually, their questions were more basic, more fundamental than the questions I was answering.

I remember one day in class when I was rattling on about the proofs for the existence of God. A student in the back row raised his hand and said, "I think we need to be honest about certain things."

"What do you have in mind?" I asked.

"Well, you seem to believe that God exists."

"Yes, I do."

"I don't."

"You don't!"

"No, I don't. And these proofs for the existence of God simply don't mean anything to me."

I was momentarily startled by his frank admission. After all, this was Wheaton College, the citadel of American evangelicalism. Who would ever think that an atheist or agnostic would be free to roam its halls of learning?

I asked, "Does anyone else agree with Steve?" To my absolute surprise several other hands slipped into the air. I was astonished, dismayed, and somewhat perplexed, to say the least.

I gave the incident some thought over the next several days and decided it was time for me to take a risk. I knew students were very troubled about the meaning of life in general. I sensed that my students were at least honest doubters. They seemed to be genuine students, willing to ask the tough questions and characterized by integrity. I came back to the next class and said, "Okay, tell me what you want to learn. Maybe I'm missing the mark by giving you all this information." I wasn't questioning my information nor my system of thought, I was simply acknowledging that my questions were not necessarily their questions and that the material was therefore irrelevant to many of them.

I was surprised when none of them seemed to have a handle on exactly what they wanted. Finally, some suggested that we discuss contemporary drama and music as a jumping off point for exploring issues of meaning: Who am I? What is the purpose of life? What gives my life meaning and significance?

We turned to issues more fundamental than those that systematic theology generally asks. We began to probe the meaning and mystery of life by tuning into the question of meaning asked by the artists of our generation. Looking in particular at the theatre of the absurd and the human loss of meaning depicted in drama, art, and music, we began to search for a more profound and deeper meaning in life. I can't say we came to adequate conclusions, but for me and most of the people in the course it was a search in faith that eventually led many of us into a deeper encounter with God in Christ through experience. Let me tell you what happened.

In the fall of the next year, 1969, the chaplain asked me to speak in chapel. Since we were close to a new year and most especially to a new decade, I decided it would be appropriate for me to address the question "Where are we evangelicals going in the 1970s?" As I pondered and meditated on the topic, it fell very naturally into two parts. The first part, I decided, would be an evaluation of contemporary culture—the kinds of attitudes that ruled my students' lives and those of so many of their generation. The second part would be the answer.

Having settled on this two-part approach to my sermon, I began, several weeks in advance, to prepare what I believed would be an important statement that would help give direction to these students. In the first part of my sermon I traced the rise of despair, the loss of meaning, and the current conviction that God was dead. Then I focused on the second part.

"What can we tell a world of despairing people?" I asked. My outline began with the typical answer. We can tell them, I said, that God created the world and that the world is, therefore, characterized by meaning. We can tell them that God created human persons in his own image. We can tell them that humanity fell away from God. We can tell them that Christ came to redeem people from their sins . . . on and on I went, sharpening up the same old answers, repeating the same propositions, delivering the same message.

As I continued to refine the answers, I asked myself, "Webber, why don't these answers do anything for you?" I wasn't questioning the truth of their content. I simply wanted to know why it was all so cold, so calculated, so rational, so *dead.* But I could come up with no alternative, so I wrote all these typical answers down on a piece of paper.

The night I finished my preparation, which was still several days before the sermon, I laid awake wondering about those answers. Why didn't the answers work? Why didn't they work for my students? For others that I knew? For myself? And how could I, I asked myself, drop these non-answering answers on more than two thousand people when I felt so uneasy about them myself?

The next morning I dragged my tired and weary body, mind, and soul to my office. I sat there at my desk and looked at those yellow, legal-sized pages of notes. I felt comfortable and pleased about the first part of the talk. I sensed that my evaluation of things was a fairly accurate picture of what was going on in the West, in the life of the students, and in my own life. But I said to myself, "Webber, you've got to be honest about those answers. You can't preach that with integrity."

I stretched my arm across the desk, picked up the sermon manuscript and separated the two parts of the sermon. I put the historical evaluation on my left and the answer on my right. I sat there in silence for a long time just looking at those two parts of the sermon. Then, in a moment of conviction, I stood to my feet, grabbed the answer part of my sermon in both hands, and vigorously crumpled the papers. Raising my right hand and arm high above my head, I tossed those answers with all my power into the wastebasket. I dropped back into my chair and sobbed for several hours. I had thrown away my answers. I had rid myself of a system in which God was comfortably contained. I had lost my security and turned my back on years of defending God's existence, his incarnation, his resurrection, and his coming again.

As I was sitting there in my chair shed of my pretension and naked before an all-powerful and mighty God, I cried out of the depth of my soul to him. "God," I cried, "where are you? Show yourself to me. Let me know that you are." I was met by an awful silence. But it was not an empty silence. It was the silence of mystery—a silence that closed the door on my answers and broke the system in which I had enslaved God. I wept and I wept.

Shortly after, my student assistant came into my office. I told him what had happened and he wept. I went to my class and told them what had happened and they wept.

The next day I stood before the student body and delivered

the first part of my sermon. Then I closed my notebook, looked at them directly, and told them what had happened to me. I told them that the answers don't work, that what we need is not answers about God, but God himself. And I told them how God was more real to me in his silence than he had been in my textbook answers. My God was no longer the God you could put on the blackboard or the God that was contained in a textbook, but a maverick who breaks the boxes we build for him. As a result of that open confession, something happened that I had never experienced before that day nor have I experienced since.

Many students along with myself identified the neat little rationalisms we were hanging on to and gave them up for an encounter with the living God. Many of us, though believers, were believers in our personal belief systems, in our cozy sets of answers, in our logical systems about God. We were placing faith in a God-substitute, a creation of our mind, an intellectualized image of God. By giving that up, by throwing it away, we were open to an encounter with God himself—a mystery that defies a complete explanation, a mystery that rises above all rational systems and pat answers. It was an cathartic experience for many of us. As one student said to me, "I felt as though a vacuum had been put in my guts and everything within me was sucked out. I feel clean and whole."

* * *

If God cannot be contained in a system where can he be encountered? I didn't know it at the time, but this experience, because it forced me to seek God seeking me, pushed me in the direction of worship and the sacraments. Since neither worship nor the sacraments were given high priority in the local evangelical churches, I had to look elsewhere. My journey into the Episcopal church and into the mystery of God's saving presence in Christ communicated through worship and the sacraments had begun.

2.

A Longing for the Experience of Worship

I spent all of my childhood and most of my adult life dreading going to church. It was the place where I was supposed to get my spiritual batteries charged and it ended up being the spiritual drain of the week. I thought the problem was me. Since I've become an Episcopalian, I've discovered that what I needed was an experience of God-centered worship. I now love to be at church.

James Stambaugh
Curator, Billy Graham Museum
Wheaton College

I have four teenage children, two girls and two boys. The boys are eighteen and twelve and the girls are sixteen and fourteen. If you have had any contact with teenagers, you can imagine what it is like in my home.

My kids are happy, healthy, normal kids who, like others their age, are crazy about music. The moment they get up in the morning, the radio or stereo is turned on. When the door opens after school, the books are dropped on the coffee table, and a record is automatically dropped on the turntable. And when we get in the car to go someplace, the radio is snapped on before the door is shut.

Now, I happen to like silence. I don't know if it's a reaction to four teenagers or whether the love of silence is simply a part of me. At any rate, when I'm traveling alone in the car, I never listen to the radio. I relish the quiet, the opportunity to be alone with myself and my thoughts.

Recently, however, I was returning from a meeting in Chicago and for some reason or another I broke my own rule and turned on the radio.

An interview was being conducted with a Harvard psychologist. I didn't get his name, but I quickly tuned into the conversation because he was discussing the issue of meaning in life— What is it that holds our life together and makes life worth living? Apparently the psychologist had published an article or book on the subject.

"I used to argue," he said, "for three important sources of meaning. Now I believe there are four." My ears picked up on this matter. I've always been interested in the quest for meaning, since my own search for meaning was stimulated by the cultural revolution of the sixties.

"In my previous article," the psychologist continued, "I suggested that meaning in life came from a relationship of love, enjoyment of work, and a fulfilling recreational and social life." I began to think about these three very basic aspects of life and listened noddingly as they were discussed. I truly felt I could agree with his assertion. Certainly to love and be loved, to see work as an extension of living and not merely something one does to earn money, and to have a group of family and friends to enjoy life with were all sources of meaning for me.

I reflected on my life and felt there were times when all three of these ingredients were present and working in harmony. But I also remembered this was not always true. There were times when only one part of my life was satisfactory and other times of deep discouragement when it seemed that nothing positive was occurring in any aspect of my life. I recalled how powerful each of these three needs were in my own life. And I sensed the craving within me to be happy and satisfied in my love, my work, and my social life. But I wondered, "What is the fourth?"

Almost on cue the psychologist said, "I now think we must add worship to this list." "Worship," he went on to say, "sets our world in order. It puts God in his proper place and puts us in right relationship to him and everything else."

This statement communicated to my inner being. Indeed, as I looked back over the course of my life for the past ten years, I saw that a motivating factor in my spiritual pilgrimage had been the quest for meaningful worship. I was longing deep down within myself for something more than I had. Something within me was pushing me toward an experience of worship, an encounter with God that was different than the plate being served in the churches where I had been involved.

As I listened to the discussion, I not only agreed with the psychologist, but I was glad I had broken my rule of silence and had listened to the radio. The psychologist helped me put my finger on the reason why I thirsted for worship. According to him, my longing was not unique or unusual. Worship is a basic need shared by all people. A need which, when fulfilled, helps make life more meaningful.

During the past few months I have interviewed a large number of evangelicals who are on the Canterbury Trail. I always ask, "Why did you choose to walk the Canterbury Trail?" Without exception, the first reason given to me is "I wanted to worship God."

It isn't that we don't have worship services in the evangelical world. We do. But some feel that what takes place in those services is not an adequate and personally meaningful experience of worship.

Early Impressions of Worship

My earliest impressions of morning worship revolved around the idea of bringing in the harvest. Members of the congregation, I believed, were expected to bring their unbelieving friends and neighbors to church to expose them to the gospel and put them in a supportive situation that would encourage a personal acceptance of Christ. My experience of worship was an evangelistic model.

During my teenage years, I remember feeling confused when a service ended without a plea to come to Christ, to rededicate one's life, or to heed the call to the mission service. The altar call was the high point of the service. Everything else—the hymns, the scripture, the prayers, and of course the special music—pointed toward the moment of decision.

This approach to morning worship was further supported by my undergraduate experience. During that time, I was told that witnessing and bringing people to Christ were the only reasons for my being and for the existence of the church. I still remember a sermon in which a well-known evangelist claimed that evangelism was the only purpose that made my vocation legitimate. He said, "It's all right for you to be a doctor, as long as you are a soul-winning doctor; it's all right for you to be a lawyer, as long as you are a soul-winning lawyer; it's all right for you to be a teacher, as long as you are a soul-winning teacher; it's all right for you to be a bricklayer, as long as you are a soul-winning bricklayer." I must have assumed that it was all right to go to worship, as long as the intent of worship was to win souls.

But I grew weary of listening to preaching and hearing soul-winning messages. I began to realize that evangelism, important as it was in the church, could not become a substitute for worship. For me, the straw that broke the camel's back occurred one summer in 1957 in a church in suburban Philadelphia. A visiting evangelist who had "preached his heart out" brought us to the final point of the meeting, the invitation. We sang all the verses of the age-old hymn "Just As I Am," but no one stepped forward. After another ten-minute plea, accompanied by threats and tears and all the psychological enticements in the book, we sang the whole hymn again. But there was no response. With a tone of absolute exasperation in his voice, the evangelist announced that he was going to count to ten. After ten, if no one responded, he would wash his hands of this church and let our blood be on our heads. He counted to ten, slowly. Then, with the air of an omniscient and all-powerful judge, he announced that he knew God was working with someone in that congregation to be saved. But, he went on to say, "It's too late, the Holy Spirit is gone, the invitation is finished, the door is closed." I watched this man of God as he stomped from the pulpit, his face flushed with anger.

I wondered about what he had done and why. I wondered if his anger was related more to his feeling of failure than to his concern for our eternal welfare. I wondered if he just wanted another notch on his salvation belt, another statistic to add to his religious bookkeeping. And I said to myself, "There has got to be more to it than this. What is worship all about anyway?"

My quest led me into an educational approach to worship. The main point of the service, I believed, was to get to the sermon. The sermon was the food that nourished the people, and transformed them. The sermon was, you might say, the main dish of the meal. It was what everyone came for, so it better be good. Whether it was by intent or by design my seminary education left me with this particular notion of worship. As a student I was told to spend at least half my week preparing for the sermon. It was to be an exegetical sermon, a challenge to the mind and heart.

I must confess that in my days as a preacher this educational mentality toward worship put me under a terrible strain. I felt that I had to perform intellectually. I felt that my sermons had to be deep, thoughtful, and original or people would simply go to another church. Later as a lay person and churchgoer, a member who came looking for food, this emphasis put me under a different kind of strain. Since I seldom found what I was looking for, I quickly became disenchanted with this kind of worship. It was a vicious circle. I knew there was something wrong about the emphasis on education. But I couldn't break out of it, either as a speaker or a worshiper. All I knew was that preaching as a substitute for worship was not where it was at for me. I didn't realize yet that I had made the church into an educational institution and that what I needed was a worshiping community.

In recent years I have observed other substitutes for worship cropping up in churches and on Christian television. One of them is the entertainment mentality—do something interesting and exciting to draw the crowds! Some of the big churches bring in the Christian superstars to attract the crowds—weightlifters, singers, models, football players . . . you name it. The attitude is that if the guest personalities are well known and Christian, they will attract a larger audience. Then, when the churches have the people's attention, they can sneak in the gospel. Good motive. Poor tactic.

Another substitute is the "possibility" mentality. In this approach to worship, the purpose is to help people recover their self-esteem. We are told, "If they can only discover their own greatness . . . If we can help them tap into their inner resources and put wings on their greatest dreams and ideas, we can help turn their negatives into positives, their clouds into rainbows, their darkness into sunlight." All of this is good. Of course, we want people to feel positive about themselves, to discover their potential, and to fulfill their greatest dreams. But shouldn't we stop for a moment and say, "Hey, what is this thing called worship all about?"

It amazes me that I went through seminary without a course in worship, without any professor asking me to address the question: What is worship all about? That's changing in evangelical seminaries now, but slowly.

My longing for a more satisfying worship grew as each route I took in worship led me to a dead end street. But after giving up the evangelistic approach to worship and after the unfulfilling experience of educational worship, I didn't know what to do next. I was running out of reasons for being at church. I remember posing the question one day to a group of my friends in an open session on the subject. After dismissing evangelistic, educational, and social reasons for being at church, the only argument we couldn't dismiss was the injunction of Hebrews: "Let us consider how to stir up one another to love and good works, not neglecting to meet together, as is the habit of some" (10:24–25). But what for, we asked? No one in the group really knew, although we all had some vague and pious notions about the need to offer worship to God. But even this, as I think about it now, much later, was something that I was supposed to do. I had replaced the idea of somebody doing something for me— evangelizing me, educating me, entertaining me—with a new focus centering around my feeble efforts to praise God and do something for him. I was thoroughly confused and, frankly, fed up with the confusion.

Two Life-changing Experiences

In the middle of this quandary two things happened to me. I visited a Roman Catholic worship service on the Saturday night before Easter and I began reading about the worship of our early Christian fathers.

I had never heard of the great Easter Vigil, an ancient service that begins on Saturday night and ends with the rising of the sun on Easter Sunday morning. (Most modern churches that still celebrate this service have reduced it to two or three hours.) But in 1972 someone mentioned it to me and urged me to attend. I was tired of singing "Up from the Grave He Arose" and pretending I was excited, so I decided to try something new. I called St. Michael's Catholic Church in Wheaton and found out the time of its Easter Vigil service. I went out of curiosity more than anything else. And I had absolutely no idea what I was getting into.

I opened the door of St. Michael's Church and stepped into the narthex only to discover that I was in total darkness, huddled with about a hundred other people. No one was talking, not even a whisper. As my eyes adjusted to the darkness I could tell we were standing in a circle around several priests and acolytes. I could smell incense, and through the dim rays of distant light, I could see the outline of the priests holding candles. In the center of the priests there seemed to be a large bowl, but I couldn't tell what it was for. So I stood there in reverent silence with everyone else, waiting for whatever was going to happen.

I didn't have to wait long. All of a sudden the bowl in the center of the group burst into a flash of light and I could see the whole narthex, all the people, and the celebrants. At the same moment a young priest with an operatic voice boomed out in a chant, "The Light of Christ," and everyone began to process into the dark church. The priests went first, holding candles lit from the source of light that was still burning. The priest leading the procession carried a large white candle, at least three feet in height and six inches in circumference. It had the symbol of the cross etched in blue on the side. Later, I learned that this was the paschal candle representing Christ who is the light of the world. The rest of us followed, and we each received a small candle that was lit at the door.

As we moved into the church, our procession stopped three more times while the celebrant chanted, "The Light of Christ." The light, although bright, only cast its lengthening shadows through the sanctuary at first, but, as each of us entered with our candles, the light from the candles increased until it filled the church with its brightness. For the next several hours we listened and responded to Scripture readings, we participated in a baptismal service, and the night ended with the celebration of the Eucharist, the great thanksgiving of the church.

I began to feel the resurrection. It was more than evidence that demanded a verdict. It was more than an intellectual proposition proving the empty tomb. I couldn't put my finger on it completely, but I sensed that there was something different, something deeper about this experience of worship than anything else I had been through. I didn't really understand it at the time, but I was experiencing the resurrection. It was no longer a hard cold fact, but a warm reality. I experienced being in the tomb and walking out of that darkness into the marvelous light, the light that conquers evil, the light that is Jesus Christ.

Because this service aroused my curiosity about worship, I turned to sources describing the early Christian worship of the fathers of the church. And I was particularly drawn to the oldest form of the Christian worship service known as the Agape feast.

The Agape feast is a meal, much like our contemporary church potluck dinners, except it includes a worship service. Biblical reference to this feast is found in Acts 2:43–47 where mention is made of "breaking bread in their homes" on a daily basis. Much later, this approach to worship was still practiced as evidenced by a reference to the love feast in Jude 1:12. Comments about this love feast are found in early Christian literature that was written well into the third century.

For these early Christians, worship must have been an event of great joy and festivity. They were celebrating the resurrection of Jesus Christ and feasting in anticipation of his return. In the context of this meal they read the Scripture, related stories about Jesus, interpreted him and his work on the cross in the light of Old Testament prophecy, urged fellow Christians to live lives that were exemplary, and brought food to be distributed to the poor of the community. They also spent time in prayer for their needs, for the needs of others, and like the prayer in the synagogue, they gave thanks to God for his provision. After they had prayed, they took bread and wine, the symbols Christ had given of his broken body and his shed blood, and as Jesus had taught, they remembered him through the celebration of the Eucharist.

I was greatly attracted to the simplicity, the power, and the warmth of this approach to worship. But the church I was attending didn't have such a practice. Since I longed to experience this reality, my family and I left the established church and began a house church modeled after the early Christian communities. About forty other people, mostly married couples from the college, joined us.

Every Sunday we met at our home. We sang, read, and interpreted the Scriptures, celebrated Holy Communion, ate a meal together, and spent most of the day in fellowship with each other.

It was an exhilarating spiritual experience at first. But it lasted less than two years because we were a small community of people separated from the larger body of Christ, isolated and alone.

I now view that experience as an important and necessary transition to worship in a more liturgical setting. It was a step toward a public worship that retained the emphasis on the Word and the breaking of the bread within the context of prayer and fellowship.

As I recognized the problems inherent in a house church and, at the same time, grew in my need for a worship that included both the Word and the Eucharist, I began thinking and praying about my next step in faith. It was at this point that my attention turned to the Episcopal church, because it retained the simple structure of worship of the early church.

My initial reaction to the more formal setting in the Episcopal church was one of confusion and uncertainty. I wasn't used to using a prayer book, responding to Scripture, praying spontaneously, singing the Lord's Prayer, saying the creed, kneeling, and receiving communion regularly. I needed to understand better what was going on and what I was doing. So I began to study the meaning of Episcopal worship. Although this is not the place to go into that study in depth, I would like to mention a few things that have helped me appreciate and embrace Episcopal worship.

A Word of Appreciation

First, I am impressed with the fact that worship in the Book of Common Prayer is directed toward God. This is evident in the first acclamation of worship: "Blessed be God, Father, Son, and Holy Spirit and Blessed be his Kingdom forever and ever." I have been put off by the narcissism of much contemporary worship. In this setting the orientation of worship appears to center around me, my feelings, and my experience, rather than around God, his person, and his work in Jesus Christ.

I am reminded of a prayer written by Hippolytus, a bishop in Rome at the beginning of the third century. In the prayer he says, "Having in memory, therefore, his death and resurrection, we offer to thee the bread and the cup, yielding thee thanks, because thou hast counted us worthy to stand before thee and to minister to thee."

The idea that worship is a ministry to God, that he loves to be worshiped, and that he made us to worship him dominates the worship of the ancient church. It is early Christian conviction drawn from Revelation 4 and 5. In these chapters, we see the heavenly host gathered around the throne in heaven, singing the praises of the Triune God.

St. John Chrysostom, a fourth-century bishop from Constantinople, describes that worship in his liturgy: "We give you thanks also for this ministry (worship and praise); vouchsafe to receive it from our hands, even though thousands of angels and ten thousand of angels stand before you, cherubim and seraphim, with six wings and many eyes, flying on high singing the triumphal hymn proclaiming, crying, and saying: 'Holy, Holy, Holy, Lord of Sabaoth; heaven and earth are full of your glory. Hosanna in the highest. Blessed is he who comes in the name of the Lord. Hosanna in the highest.' " When I worship I too feel lifted up into the heavenly host. I join them in the praise and worship of Almighty God, Father, Son, and Holy Spirit.

Second, I am impressed with the Christ-centered nature of worship in the Book of Common Prayer. The central thrust of worship in the Episcopal tradition, just as it was in the ancient tradition, is to celebrate Jesus Christ as the central cosmic figure of the universe. The prayer of thanksgiving at the Eucharist, for example, is modeled after the vision of the world set forth in

Scriptures and summarized by Paul in Colossians 1. It recounts creation, the fall, the coming of Jesus in the womb of the virgin, his life, death, burial, resurrection, and coming again as the reason for the great thanksgiving.

Whenever I hear this prayer, I repeat the words silently and allow my imagination to picture everything from the creation to the consummation. The prayer itself and the whole Eucharistic action is a majestic rehearsal of the role Christ has played in creating and recreating the world. During this prayer, I am always moved to give thanks to God for the work of Christ, because I feel the benefit of his death and resurrection is being conveyed to me in a fresh experience of spiritual healing. The mystery of his passion wraps around me, penetrates into my very inner person, cleanses me of my sin, restores my relationship to God, and nourishes me in the faith. Worship has become a kind of evangelistic experience for me, extending the benefits of Christ's death and resurrection to me again and again.

I also appreciate the emphasis on Scripture reading in the Episcopal tradition. In the early church, when there were no Bibles, the reading of Scripture often lasted several hours. In contemporary worship there is much less reading, but the Episcopal church has retained at least three readings and a psalm. This is more Scripture than most churches read on a typical Sunday morning. And, because the lectionary is followed, a central theme pertaining to the season of the church year runs through the Scripture lessons. Usually, the sermon is also related to that biblical theme.

For this reason I have found that the worship of the Episcopal church gives direction to my spiritual life. The Scripture readings and theme of the week bring me into a relationship with Christ's life in such a way that I experience the mystery of his passion. During Advent, for example, I am drawn into the mystery of awaiting his coming. Simeon's expression of the anticipation of seeing the Messiah becomes my own longing as my devotion to Christ awaits his birth in Bethlehem.

As I meditate on my worship experience in the Episcopal tradition, I find that I am drawn to it because it is so thoroughly evangelical. I have always confessed Christ as the central person of human history and of my life. Yet, until my worship life was oriented around an ordered experience of Christ not only on a weekly, but on a yearly pattern, I was unable to express in a concrete way my personal commitment to Christ. Weekly worship and the calendar of the sacred year gives direction and definition to my spiritual life. I no longer walk alone as in a lone-ranger Christianity, but I join with millions of Christians around the world in a weekly and yearly devotion that defines our existence in the world.

* * *

Now the question is: Is there something from this ancient historic tradition of worship that can benefit the evangelical tradition? I think so.

Evangelical worship, for the most part, centers on the preacher. What he says to us, how he says it, and what effect his words have on us appear to be paramount. In seminary the pastor has probably been trained to think that worship centers around him. And years of centering worship around the pastor and his sermon has conditioned the people to expect it and want it. But we have to ask whether or not pastor-centered worship is right and biblical. The evidence of 1 Corinthians 12 and the historical pattern prior to the Reformation era certainly speak against it. And many more people today are becoming increasingly dissatisfied with a pastor-dominated worship experience.

I have discovered that a major reason why people are leaving evangelical churches for Episcopal churches is their longing for a more satisfying experience of worship. Maybe the key to satisfaction within the Evangelical tradition can be found by restoring a worship in which Christ is front center not only in our weekly worship, but in our pattern of yearly personal and corporate worship as well.

3.

A Desire for Sacramental Reality

───────────────◆───────────────

In the sacrament of the Eucharist I feel close to the Lord, almost like he's saying, "I'm here." I re-experience Jesus—his death and resurrection. It's almost like having somebody over for dinner. It's a real tight friendship. My relationship to him is cemented in the fact that he comes close to me in the bread and wine.

Lou Ann Elwell
Counselor of
Wheaton College Students

In the fall of 1974 I was deeply concerned about my future church affiliation. I was in a crisis situation. I had already acknowledged to myself that continuation in an independent house church was no longer an option for me. The feeling of isolation from the Body of Christ was becoming more intense, and I needed to make a decision.

I remember walking across campus one sunny afternoon, with my hands in my pockets, my head hanging forward, and my eyes glued to the sidewalk. I was wrestling myself. Who am I spiritually? With whom is my identity? To whom do I belong?

These questions were churning within me when I bumped into Leanne Payne, a charismatic Episcopal deaconness. I knew her fairly well because we had discussed many things together, including the Episcopal church.

She took one look at me and said, "Bob, what's the matter with you? You look deeply troubled. I see strain in your face and in your eyes."

"You're right," I said and I spilled out my concern over church affiliation.

"Bob," Leanne responded, "let's go to your office and pray."

"Sure," I agreed, without knowing what I was getting into. I assumed she meant to pray like most people pray with each other—bow your head and offer your petition to the Lord.

But Leanne had something else in mind. As we stepped into my office she said, "Sit down and relax. While you pray quietly, I'm going to lock the door and turn off the light because I don't want anybody walking in on us."

I watched with curiosity as she drew a small silver vial from her pocketbook. She made the sign of the cross over the vial and uttered a brief prayer to set the oil apart as an agent of the Holy Spirit. Then she dipped her thumb into the precious oil and placed that oil on my head in the sign of the cross and in the name of the Father, the Son, and the Holy Spirit.

"Bob," she said, "we are going to do the healing of memories for you and ask God to give you a clear direction in your life." She clasped her hands around the sides of my head and encouraged me to pray through every stage of my spiritual journey. Starting in my pre-school years through high school, college, and seminary, we prayed through my spiritual journey, asking God for a sense of direction. I began to feel a sense of release from the past. To this day the effects of that prayer are still with me. For the confusion about my spiritual identity was laid to rest, and my feeling of being drawn into the Episcopal church was confirmed.

This incident points to the basic sacramental principle: God works through life, through people, and through physical, tangible, and material reality to communicate his healing presence in our lives. The point is that God does not meet us outside of life in an esoteric manner. Rather, he meets us through life incidents, and particularly through the sacraments of the church. Sacrament, then, is a way of encountering the mystery.

A Non-Sacramental Background

I grew up with the view that sacraments were akin to magic. It's not that I knew what the sacraments were. I don't think I could have named them or said anything about their meaning at all. I simply thought of them as part of the liturgy, practiced especially among the Catholics. It was my impression that Catholics looked upon the sacraments as the means to get to heaven. Just get baptized, take the Eucharist, go to confession once in a while, and salvation is guaranteed. If you had asked me whether faith or a spiritual life were part of salvation in the liturgical tradition, I would have said, "No, just take the sacraments and all will be well."

In spite of my superficial view of the sacraments, I did have a strong sense of the importance of baptism and the Lord's Supper in my own experience. My own baptism at age thirteen was not something that was perfunctory. I can still remember the day my father talked to me about my need to be baptized. I was sitting in the kitchen of the Baptist parsonage where we lived, snacking on cookies and drinking a Coke. My father slipped into a chair beside me and said, "Robert, I'm going to be conducting some classes for people who will be baptized this spring. Now that you're thirteen, I think it's time you give serious consideration to the step of baptism. By being baptized you will be making a public confession that you do believe in Christ and that you are willing to follow him." I remember going out on the back porch that night, looking up into the stars, and asking myself whether or not I really believed, whether or not I was

willing to take up my cross and follow after Christ. The prospect
of my own baptism caused me to choose Christ again in a more
intense way, to determine once more to follow him.

I also remember the seriousness with which I received the
Lord's Supper. On the first Sunday of every month we received
the bread and wine in a most solemn ceremony. The communion table was always covered with a recently washed and
ironed linen cloth, neatly laid over the stack of communion
trays. The plates of bread were carefully placed on either side of
these trays. Behind the table, there were enough chairs for my
father, the pastor, the deacons, and one empty chair symbolizing
Christ's presence. The somber sermon, hymns, and prayers almost always focused on the death of Christ. Then before communion was served, it was made clear that everyone should prepare by repenting his or her sins. I can remember how seriously
I took this admonition, how I always repented of unknown sins,
and how fearful I was of eating and drinking unworthily, damn-
ing myself out of a relationship with God.

Allow me to step out of my memory for a moment and comment on my early perceptions of the sacraments. First, as I will
expand on later, I had an extremely limited view of the sacraments. I had no sense of how the concept of sacrament—encountering the mystery—could be related to all of life. Even
though I frequently encountered God's will for my life in events
and through people, I didn't acknowledge my experiences as
sacramental. And even through I knew that all of life needed to
be related to God, I wasn't aware that I longed for a name to
attach to this conviction.

Second, I not only misunderstood the liturgical tradition in
regard to baptism and the Lord's Supper, but I even misunderstood my own practice. I thought the liturgical view was that
God gave salvation through the sacraments, separate from the
faith of the recipient. And I viewed my own practice of baptism
and the Lord's Supper as if everything depended on me. On
both counts I was wrong. I had failed to recognize that the
liturgical tradition calls upon the recipient to have faith, and
that, in my Baptist experience, the energy of spiritual fusion
with God wasn't coming completely from me. God was really
there acting in the baptismal water and in the bread and wine.
In retrospect, I realize I had faith, but I lacked the understand-

ing that God works through tangible and visible means to communicate his healing presence. Nevertheless, my Baptist background prepared me to become sacramental.

Becoming Sacramental

Because of my Baptist background, the words "becoming sacramental" still have an odd ring. And on occasion a red flag goes up in response to such words as liturgical or Eucharist. But these words go back to early Christian vocabulary, and they carry many connotations. Let me try to explain what the idea of sacrament is and why I find the sacramental dimension of the church to be a compelling spiritual force in my life.

As we have seen, a primary meaning of sacrament is that God works through his created order, through visible and tangible signs. For example, signs like water, bread, wine, oil, and the laying on of hands are visible and tangible meeting points between God and people. They are the points of intersection between God's action and human faith. I haven't always believed this principle. There was a time I would have tossed this idea out as heretical. I would have insisted that God always communicates spirit to spirit—his spirit with my spirit. I would have dismissed any hint of a visible or tangible sign of this meeting as dangerous and non-biblical. But I changed my mind for two reasons.

First, I've become sacramental because of the incarnation. I've always believed God became human. But not until ten years ago did I begin to wrestle with the implication of the incarnation. The incarnation affirms that God became one of us. He entered into our flesh and blood experience. I tell my students that the litmus test for orthodoxy is found in the answer to the following question: "Pinch Jesus, and what does he say?" The obvious answer is, "Ouch." He was a real person, just like us, sin excepted.

Now, although I always believed Jesus was human, I never really thought the idea through. The point, of course, is that God became present to his world not in a spiritual, bodiless, timeless, spaceless way. Rather, he became human in flesh and blood, in time, space, and history. The incarnation affirms that God acted through material creation to give us his salvation.

Here then is the sacramental principle again! God uses his created order as a vehicle of his saving, comforting, and healing presence.

John Calvin, the great Protestant Reformer, captured this sacramental principle rather well when he wrote in the *Christian Institutes* that "our ignorance and slothfulness, and, I may add, the vanity of our minds, require external aids, in order to the production of faith in our hearts, and its increase and progressive advance even to its completion, God has provided such aids." Once I was willing to give up a spiritual spirituality and accept a spirituality rooted in creation and incarnation, in mundane things like water, oil, bread, and wine, as well as in people and incidents, I was on the road to becoming sacramental.

Gaining a better understanding of the early church fathers' use of the word *sacrament* also helped my journey toward becoming sacramental. The word *sacramentum,* I discovered, is a Latin word derived from two root meanings. The word *sacra* means "holy" and the suffix *mentum* means "to make." So the earliest usage of the word is "to make holy." I didn't find that objectionable at all. I began to see that the sacraments, these visible and tangible signs, were means by which my relationship with God in faith was established, repaired, and maintained.

As I read more extensively writers like Tertullian, Irenaeus and Cyprian, Augustine, Ambrose, Athanasius, St. John Chrysostom, and other early church fathers, I became less and less prejudiced. Rather than encountering a pagan idea, I discovered what seemed to me to be a thoroughly evangelical concept of the word.

For example, I was surprised to discover that these fathers thought in terms of one sacrament—one visible, tangible means by which we are brought to God. That means is Jesus Christ. He is *the* sacrament *par excellence.* The fathers never argued for salvation by the sacraments. Rather, the sacraments of water and bread and wine, they said, are the visible, tangible signs of Christ's saving action. The purpose of the sacrament is to signify Christ and thus provide a sign of his encounter with us.

Consequently, the fathers saw many things as sacramental. They recognized many means by which Christ's saving reality was signified. Tertullian, for example, went back to the Old Testament and saw sacramental signs everywhere: the Exodus is sacramental because it points to the Christ event; the offices of prophet, priest, and king are sacramental because they are ful-filled in Christ, who as prophet speaks the Word of God, as priest intercedes for us, and as king rules over his creation. Even the Tabernacle and the Temple, with all their sacrifices and sa-cred rituals, were seen as sacramental. Surely, the Book of He-brews interprets the Temple and its religious functions as point-ing to Christ and being fulfilled in him. What is important here is that all these visible, tangible, and concrete realities were shadows of what was to come. They looked to Jesus, the person whose reality they signified.

When the early fathers evaluated the New Testament church, they saw that it, like the Old Testament, also contained sacra-ments, that is, visible signs that take us to Jesus. They spoke not only of baptism and the Lord's Supper as visible means by which we are brought to Christ, but also of the Gospels, prayer, the study of doctrine, and the power of a life led as a good example.

I found myself highly attracted to this understanding of the sacraments because it is so Christ-centered. But I had to come to grips with the idea that a supernatural Christianity based on "God with us" in Jesus Christ and a sacramental Christianity that recognizes God's continued presence with us in the church through visible signs are really two sides of the same coin. Actu-ally, I discovered that this sacramental sense is not as far re-moved from my evangelical background as it first appeared. I had always believed the Scriptures somehow mysteriously repre-sented the means through which God became present to the reader. All I had to do was extend this principle to all of life and to specific signs of God's acting in the church.

A Sacramental Viewpoint

I have already mentioned that my pilgrimage into the liturgi-cal church was related to my concern for rediscovering mystery. I'm no longer willing to look at my world through the eyes of Enlightenment rationalism. I'm convinced that there is more to life than what can be seen by the naked eye, by literalism, or by reason. A conviction to the supernatural calls me to see what is behind the literal, to penetrate more deeply into the mystery of life.

A sacramental view of life is not much different from a supernatural view of life. It affirms the mystery of the universe and allows that everything in life is, in one way or another, related to the mystery of the Creator and Redeemer. For example, I once saw a poster on which were written the words of a Catholic thinker, Teilhard de Chardin: "Because of creation and even more because of incarnation there is nothing profane for those who know how to see." That's it, I said to myself, that phrase captures the broadest sense of sacrament. Because God created this world and even more because he actually became his creation, creation itself—its material substance, its history, its events, and even my small history within the whole—is not profane or secular. There is a religious underpinning to life, a purpose to everything, an end when all things will work out all right. Therefore, everything in life points to the center, to Christ the Creator and Redeemer in whom all things—visible and invisible—find their meaning. That's sacrament in its broadest sense. As an Evangelical, I already believed this. I simply had not recognized that this was a sacramental view of life. Now I had a name for it.

I also discovered that the idea of sacrament relates to the church. Although all of life is sacred, there is something in life that has the specific function of taking us to Christ, and that is his church. The church is the sign of Christ's redemption; it is the mother of those who would have God as their Father. In the womb of the church we are born to eternal life, and in the arms of the church we are nurtured and carried to safety. So the church, that community of God's people on earth, is sacramental because it takes us to Christ.

And God has given the church specific signs through which he acts to save us, to help us, and to lead us in faith. The two most important signs, clearly taught by Jesus, are baptism and the Eucharist. Baptism is the sign of our entrance into the church, and the Eucharist is the visible reminder that the only way to God is through the broken body and blood of his son Jesus Christ. By receiving the bread and wine, we are continually fed and nourished, for they bring Christ's action on the cross to us again and again. His work is not repeated. Rather, the application of his work is continually made real as we, in faith, add our "Amen," our "So be it," our "Yes" of acceptance to his recreating and renewing work.

In this view, the sacrament is not a thing in itself, an end, but

a means through which Christ encounters us savingly. I'm reminded of a sermon preached by an Episcopal rector at a baptism. He looked the congregation squarely in the eye and said,
"I want to remind you, water does not save, only Christ saves.
This water," he went on to say, "is the sign of his saving action,
the concrete manifestation of his love and acceptance, offered to
those who come for baptism."

I find the presence of Christ to be particularly true for me in
the sacrament of the Eucharist. When I used to think of it as my
personal sign of faith, I always wondered, "Did I take it in the
right way? Did I properly prepare myself through the confession
of my sins to make myself worthy of the bread and wine? Was
my faith strong enough to be pleasing to God? Will his wrath
come against me because I wasn't serious enough?" All these
worries rolled away when I was set free by understanding that
the bread and wine are God's symbols of his love toward me.
They now speak to me of the mystery of my salvation. Rather
than sending me into myself in search of this or that sin to
confess, the Eucharist makes me aware that I never have been
and never will be worthy. But more than that, the Eucharist tells
me that I am acceptable to God because of Jesus Christ. He has
done all that needs to be done to make me acceptable to the
Father. This is his sign to me of his work for me. I receive this
sign in faith and it effects a healing with God, my neighbor,
nature, and me. What Christ did for me on the cross is now
extended to me. I receive the benefits of his salvation again and
again. So the Eucharist has become the sacrament of my encounter with Jesus Christ. He who saved me at the cross continues to extend his salvation to me through the simple and concrete signs of bread and wine.

The above illustrations remind me of how the early church's
approach to the sacraments differed from my earlier views. As I
mentioned before, I had looked on the sacraments as *my* sign of
faith directed toward God. My impression was that I could
show God that I loved him by being baptized and by eating the
bread and drinking the wine. But the early church, and with
them the Reformers, presented the sacraments as God's signs,
not ours. In and through them God actively conveys himself and
his grace. They are his signs, and as I participate in faith, my
relationship with him is established, repaired, and maintained.

In history the church has also identified other specific ways in which God's saving grace in Christ is visibly manifest. These are found in the rites of confirmation, confession, marriage, holy orders, and unction. In each of these events God's grace is present in a very special way to provide assistance in the journey of faith and to meet us in a tangible way.

For example, the sacrament of confirmation is really not an invention of the medieval church. Its biblical root goes all the way back to the reception of the Holy Spirit by the primitive Christian community, described in Acts. Paul, in Ephesians 1:13, makes reference to our "seal by the Holy Spirit." I remember when I knelt before the bishop who placed oil on my forehead and then, clasping his hands on my head, prayed, "Strengthen, O Lord, your servant Robert with your Holy Spirit; empower him for your service, and sustain him all the days of his life. Amen." He then slapped me on the face to remind me that "in this world you will have persecution for Christ's sake." I didn't look at that experience as the moment I received the Holy Spirit. Rather, I looked at it as the sign given by God that the Holy Spirit was given to me.

If I ever doubt God's work of grace for me, my memory of the external act of confirmation is a perpetual reminder that I have been brought into the community of Christ and that I am called to live in the mystery of this relationship with the Triune God and with his people, the church. The fact that this is God's sign to me, rather than my sign to him, in no way detracts from my experience of faith. If anything, it encourages and enriches my faith and trust in God. To me it is a thoroughly evangelical sacrament. It brings me to God, to faith in him and his work for me.

I also find the sacrament of confession, now known as the rite of reconciliation, to be thoroughly biblical and evangelical in meaning. Certainly St. John calls us to confession when he says, "If we confess our sins, he is faithful and just, and will forgive our sins and cleanse us from all unrighteousness" (1 John 1:9). In my evangelical background the confession of sin played an important role in my spiritual pilgrimage. I now see the importance of confession as a sacrament, that is, confession through another person. This person, whether a minister, a friend, or a spiritual director, bears the responsibility of holding the confessor accountable.

I have always heard objections to confessing your sins to another person. I've been told that it is much better to go directly to God, because no other person has the power to forgive your sins. This perception of confession contains some misinformation. I remember how I carried fears based on those objections into my first confession only to have them quickly destroyed.

The purpose of confessing sins to another person has to do with accountability. When we sin, we not only sin against God, but against ourselves and our neighbor. Therefore, it makes sense to confess to God in the sight and hearing of another human who can hold us accountable for our lives. Further, no person himself forgives us. He or she, acting in the name of Christ, simply assures us that when we confess our sins in faith, trusting in God to forgive us, we indeed are forgiven and enter a healing stage. The one to whom we confess is a visible and personal agent of God who proclaims what God promises. In this proclamation we are again reminded of the mystery of redemption: it is God who saves us and heals us and brings us to himself.

Marriage has also been identified as a sacrament because it is understood by Paul in the light of the relationship that exists between Christ and the church. Marriage is a concrete situation in which the love that exists between Christ and the church may be exemplified. There is a sacred bond in marriage. It is not merely a human agreement between two people, but an agreement that is to be lived in the context of covenantal commitment. Christ has taken the church to be his bride, to love and cherish as his own body. Marriage is characterized by this kind of commitment. In this day of easy relationships when some turn in a spouse as one would turn in a car, there is a greater need for a truly sacramental concept of an agreement as unique as marriage.

Holy orders or ordination also have come to be acknowledged as a sacrament. Here, in this office in which one has been called to do the work of ministry, God's action is being demonstrated. It is, of course, not for everyone. Rather, it is only for those who are called by God to minister in his church. To regard holy orders as a sacrament does not deny the priesthood of all believers, a cardinal point of the Reformers. Rather, it affirms that an ordinary member of the church has been given the particular responsibility of handling the Word of God and the administration of the sacraments. In this action the office holder represents Jesus Christ. The old caricature that a priest is a mediator between people and God and therefore denies or usurps the ministry of Christ in the church is not true. In my experience the function of the priest in the Anglican tradition is to be the human representative of God. I find, for example, that a godly priest or minister inspires and motivates me toward holiness. I have experienced a shepherding relationship from the priests of the Anglican tradition. I find that a spiritual father, a director of my spiritual life, a person to whom I am accountable for my rule of prayer and Christian life is helpful in giving me personal spiritual direction.

Another sacrament identified by the church is the sacrament of unction. I've already described my experience with this sacrament when I recalled the day Leanne Payne prayed with me. My earliest introduction to this sacrament was related to death. In the medieval church unction was the sacrament of death rather than the sacrament for wholeness and health. The old view of this sacrament is that it is administered to the dying as they leave this world to assure them of salvation. Since Vatican II, the healing dimension of this sacrament, which is rooted in James 5:12 where the elders are instructed to anoint the sick with oil and pray for them, has been restored.

Recovering a Supernatural Christianity

But why are all these sacraments important to me? Why do I want something more than the immediate relationship to God established by the new birth? Isn't what I had in the evangelical tradition enough?

I am reminded of a comment made by a minister in the Episcopal church who was being interviewed for an appointment at St. Barnabas Church in Glen Ellyn. He had been a minister in another Protestant tradition. The question was asked, "Why did you leave your church background to become an Episcopal minister?" I will never forget his answer because it helped me identify one of the aspects of the Episcopal tradition that I found especially helpful in my spiritual journey.

He answered, "I was frustrated as a minister in the free-church tradition because I didn't have adequate tools with which to deal with the problems of my people."

"What, for example?"

"Well, I often visited the sick in hospitals or at home and always felt it was not enough to simply read the Scripture and pray with them."

"What else did you want to do?"

"I wanted to offer them a visible and tangible sign of God's power. I wanted to touch them with something real and definite."

"Can you give us an example?"

"Yes, I wanted to be able to take the oil of unction and put it on their heads with the sign of the cross. I think that's a touch from God that adds something to Scripture reading and a Psalm. But my church frowned on the practice."

I was reminded of my own stay in the hospital when my minister came by and simply prayed for me. I wanted more than that; I wanted to be touched by God and to be left with something specific that conveyed God's action for me in the then and now.

The conversation with the candidate for St. Barnabas also reminded me of a tragic occurrence in the life of one of my former students. This young man graduated from Wheaton College, then from an east coast seminary, and later became a pastor in a small town in Pennsylvania. During the first year of his pastorate, he was diagnosed as having cancer. While in the hospital, he asked the elders of the church where he was pastor to anoint him with oil and pray for him. But they would not because they still believed the old concept that the sacraments were magical. For them, anointing with oil was Catholic and pagan. My friend had to ask the pastor and elders of another church to come and anoint him.

I have found in the past I too was a supernaturalist when it came to the inspiration of the Bible, the deity and resurrection of Jesus, and personal conversion. The practical supernatural dimension of the Christian faith in the sacraments was rejected by me as superstition. I no longer regard the sacraments as magical or pagan. Rather, I have come to believe they are visible means through which the saving and healing action of God through Jesus Christ is communicated to his people. The sacraments do not save us. They are vehicles through which the salvation of the world accomplished by Christ is extended to us. They bring Christ to us and touch us with his healing power.

* * *

I am persuaded by my own experience and my study of the use of the sacraments that they provide us with a way to truly touch people with the power of Christ.

I do not deny the power of the Holy Spirit working more directly. But I am interested in the fact that our evangelical approach to being born again stands in the tradition of a sacrament. We insist on some external acts which visibly portray the power of Christ to convert the person. When we ask someone to raise his hand for salvation, or stand up and walk the aisle, we are describing a sacramental action.

God communicates to us through visible and tangible means. He came to us in an enfleshed form. He was made man and lived among us. Now he continues to act in our lives through those symbols we call sacraments. I can only testify to the power of that experience as one that continually keeps me in Christ and the church.

4.

The Search for Spiritual Identity

In the past I felt as though Christianity began a few years before I became a Christian. I began to sense a real need to belong to my Christian heritage. When I became an Episcopalian, I added a new dimension to my faith that I had never experienced before. I now feel my connection with all those Christians that have gone before me.

Melody Patterson
Graduate of Oral Roberts University
and Wheaton Graduate School

You will probably remember the celebrated case of Jane Doe. In 1980, Jane, a blonde woman about thirty-eight years old who was physically attractive and endowed with a sound and intelligent mind, turned up in Florida without a hint of who she was.

I remember reading about her in the papers and watching her on television as an all out nationwide search was made for her identity. I couldn't fully understand her dilemma because I have always known who I am. I've always been claimed by my parents and have a sense of continuity with my past through my friends and my memory of the schools, events, and people who have shaped my life.

I did, however, allow myself to imagine the frustration that Jane must have experienced, being fully alert to her immediate surroundings but having no recall whatsoever of her parents, childhood, education, work, friends, or anything else in her life.

Jane Doe was a woman in search of an identity. She desperately wanted to know who she was and to whom she belonged.

Although I have never suffered from amnesia in the technical, medical sense, I do think one of the reasons I moved in the direction of the Episcopal church was my strong desire to find a historical identity. I wanted to belong to church history—to feel myself a part of the past. I wanted to stand in the tradition of those who had gone before me. I felt separated from the past and conscious only of my immediate present. From my conversations with other evangelicals who have moved into the Episcopal church, I have discovered that my search for a historical identity with the church through the ages is a concern shared by others on the same journey.

The Apostate Church

As far back as I can remember I was told that the "established" church was apostate. By established church I don't mean the Catholic or Orthodox church. The apostate nature of these churches was taken for granted. It was my impression that these were pagan perversions of the truth. And it was clear that anyone who was converted from one of those traditions would leave immediately. Staying in the Catholic church was not an option or a matter of discussion. Occasionally, a converted Catholic would speak in church and confirm all these suspicions.

But, for me, the immediate issue of apostasy that was relevant and close at hand had to do with the main-line Protestant church. I was told that it was a clear-cut truth that the Episcopal, Lutheran, Presbyterian, and Methodist churches, to name a few, were beyond hope. They were social clubs filled with liberals, modernists, and apostles of evil. The phrase in Revelation "come out from among them and be ye separate" was applied to the true Christian's relationship to one of these bodies. Real Christians left these centers of abomination.

I still recall the day in the spring of 1945 when two establishment leaders from the American Baptist Convention came to talk with my father, then pastor of the Montgomeryville Baptist Church in Montgomeryville, Pennsylvania. My father, I was told by my mother, was too conservative for the American Baptist Convention. And now, these apostate leaders of the church were putting pressure on my father and other conservatives like him to either change their antiquated views or leave the church.

I sensed that we were martyrs for the truth, that Satan was working through these two ominous-looking men to destroy the truth. I began to feel it was "us" against "them" and I felt proud and confirmed in my Gideon-like complex when my father left the American Baptist Convention and affiliated with the Conservative Baptist denomination.

My sense of standing alone against the tide of doctrinal and spiritual corruption was increased during my undergraduate years. During this time, I was introduced to the "Trail of Blood" theory. True Christians, it was argued, always stood outside the established church. The identity of a modern Christian who was *truly* Christian was with those persons and groups who had been put out of the church, even martyred for the sake of their stand for the faith.

I understood the concept, but still failed to have any identity because no one informed me about these people. Who they were and exactly what they represented remained a mystery to me. I simply knew that to suffer the reproach of being "outside" the main stream of Christianity was somehow the experience of all the true Christians who preceded me.

A Protestant Identity

As I proceeded with my walk through history, I felt that my identity had to be connected somewhere in the Protestant tradition. I wondered if I could find a home with Luther, with Calvin, or with the Anabaptists. I was particularly attracted to John Calvin. I liked his commentaries and his system of thought so clearly laid out in the *Institutes*. Here was a clear mind, a warm heart, a great leader of the church. I could start with him, I thought.

At the Reformed Episcopal Seminary in Philadelphia, I studied under Robert K. Rudolf, a master teacher and a walking encyclopedia of Calvinist theology. By his magnetic personality and his deep devotion to logically consistent truths I was soon drawn into the teaching of John Calvin. I thought, "here it is." I swallowed it whole. As I look back on that experience, it was as though I thought God himself had given John Calvin the final, ultimate, complete, and authoritative interpretation of the Bible.

I now had an identity. I belonged, as it were, to the family of Calvinists, that great body of people who referred all questions to the great systematic mind of Calvin. If a question came up, no matter what it was, the method of answering that question was always, "What did Calvin say?" I soon found it was unhealthy to disagree with Calvin or to question his interpretation on any given subject.

I began to suspect that the reason why it was unhealthy to question Calvin was a matter of security. After all, Calvin was not only my ticket to knowing the truth, he was also my means of being able to judge those who didn't agree with me.

My special glee was to put the Arminians down (Arminius called Calvin's theology into question and began an opposite tradition of interpretation known as Arminianism. This view point is strongly held among the Wesleyan, Pentecostal groups, and the Holiness Tradition in general). I was also able to distinguish myself from the Lutherans. They were a bit too Catholic, their break from Rome was inadequate. It didn't go far enough. As the Puritans were to say of both Lutherans and Anglicans, they retained "rags of popery." I was also able to set myself against the Anabaptists (Mennonites and Brethren come from them), especially because of their pacifism.

All of this worked very neatly for me and I felt most comfortable with it until I actually met Arminians, Lutherans, Anabaptists, and Roman Catholics who were devout Christian people. The neat little lines I had drawn to assure my identity were beginning to crumble. The problem as I see it now is that I had gained my identity through an association with a particular historical tradition. I think it would have been appropriate to accuse me of being a Calvinist first and a Christian second. I never would have admitted it, but the fact is that this was true.

My search for an identity took on a whole new perspective in my graduate program. There were two experiences in particular that stretched me and helped my search for identity to begin to come to closure. Let me tell you about them.

Two Experiences

First of all, I enrolled in a course entitled "The Apostolic Fathers." I chose the course because it met at a convenient time and fulfilled a requirement. Little did I know that the short quarter course would arouse an interest in me, that now, more than twenty years later, is still not satiated.

The Apostolic Fathers are Christian leaders in the church who wrote and pastored churches between 100 and 150 A.D. These include men like Clement, the Bishop of Rome who wrote a letter to the church at Corinth appropriately called the first letter of Clement in 96 A.D.; the seven short letters of Ignatius, Bishop of Antioch who wrote to various churches en route to Rome where he was to be put to death in the Colosseum for his faith; and the *Didache*, a short teaching manual designed to guide early Christian ethical instruction and practices such as baptism and the Agape feast. (There are several others. But these three influenced me most.)

What was important to me from these writings and writers was not only their thought, but the sense of a *link*—a link with the apostles. These writers were actually contemporaries of the apostles, people who grew up at a time when John, for example, was still living and active in the church. They were children when some of the New Testament materials like the Gospels were written.

For me, the dawning sense of a link with primitive Christianity was exhilarating. It set in motion a whole new perception for me, a perception that made me want to march through history as it happened. I had always looked back on the history of the Church in a judgmental manner. Somehow, I felt that where I was in time and space was *better* than where anyone else had been. Now, because of the link with the apostles, I wanted to stand within history and march forward. I felt like I had found my family tree in the attic. I had this overwhelming urge to discover for the first time my Christian lineage.

Actually, this experience was quite revolutionary. Even though I was in graduate school, I was of the opinion that the church had gone apostate around 100 A.D., at the close of the New Testament age, and wasn't recovered again until the Reformation.

I was of the opinion that apostasy was the order of the day immediately in the church. I know this may appear to be an unintelligent view for someone who had already graduated from seminary. However, at that time evangelical seminaries taught very little church history and placed no emphasis on the church prior to the Reformation. Consequently, my exposure to the church prior to the Reformation was minimal and entirely deficient. For that reason, the myth of an Apostate church from the very beginning was never really addressed. That history, it was assumed, belonged to the Catholics and the Orthodox, and everyone knew that they were questionable expressions of the Christian faith. So, why bother to study people or a movement that was wrong from the start?

The second incident which happened during my graduate studies in seminary and one which was to have far reaching implications for my own spiritual pilgrimage, resulted from interest shown in me by one of my teachers, Dr. John Damm. One day after class Professor Damm said, "Bob, there are a few of us here who are interested in putting together an ecumenical fellowship group. Would you be interested in joining?" "Oh," I said, "that does sound interesting. Who would be involved?" "Well," said John, "myself and a few seminarians from Concordia; a few people from Eden Seminary, and a small handful of Catholic seminarians and priests." I gulped when I heard his last phrase. *A small handful of Catholic seminarians and priests,* I thought. All of a sudden all the images and caricatures of Romanism came to mind. How could I, a dyed-in-the-wool evangelical, a Christian committed to Protestant Christianity, have anything in common with a Roman Catholic? How could we pray together, read and discuss the Scripture and fellowship together? Can Jerusalem and Babylon have anything in common?

Dr. Damm raised this question with me in 1965, the year that Vatican II came to an end. Pope John XXIII had opened the windows of the Roman church and had invited fresh winds to blow through the structure. Little did I know that those winds would also blow on me and assist my pilgrimage into an identity with the universal church.

After thinking over the proposal made by my professor, I decided that, threatened as I was by a Catholic presence, it would at least be an interesting experience to have firsthand contact with a few Roman Catholics. My aunt was a Catholic, but it was something that we never discussed in her presence. Other than my aunt I had never had any personal contact with a Catholic, let alone prayer with a priest. Nevertheless, I decided to grit my spiritual teeth and endure the pain. Maybe, I thought, I could be a witness to these pagans and help them come to a saving knowledge of Christ.

I went to the first meeting with great apprehension and defensiveness. Would these Mary-worshipers, these advocates of works righteousness, these saint-worshipers, and pray-ers for the dead know anything about true Christianity? Would they be so steeped in tradition, so warped by liturgy, and so attached to their beads that discussion of Scripture, personal prayer, and fellowship would be foreign to their experience?

That first evening together was an evening I will never forget. We decided to sit in a circle and share our faith pilgrimages with each other. I still remember one of the seminarians. He was a young blond, short of stature with a boyish face, a disarming grin, and a brilliant mind. I don't remember his name, but I recall that he was a philosophy major, a candidate for a Ph.D. at St. Louis University. He began speaking. "Jesus Christ," he said, "means everything to me. He is my Lord, my Savior, my friend. I want to tell you how I met him." In warm and glowing terms, he shared his faith in Jesus and spoke of his love of the Scriptures, his life of prayer, and his concern to get to know Christians from other traditions. His love for Christ and the church was catching, as was the love expressed by the other Catholic seminarians and priests.

As time went on my prejudices against the Roman Catholics began to fall by the wayside. I had encountered real people who were deeply committed to Christ and his church—people who expressed their faith in a tradition different than mine, but people whom I had to admit challenged me in my own faith experience. I felt that they loved Christ more than I did, that they knew more about the Christian faith than I did, that they cared deeply about prayer and spirituality, and that they were deeply devoted to the poor, the hungry, and the outcasts of this world.

I don't mean to suggest that all Catholics are exactly like these seminarians. But there is one thing I have become convinced of. It is this: evangelical Christians do not have a monopoly on the faith. God has his people in every expression of the faith—Catholic, Orthodox, Protestant, fundamentalist, evangelical, Holiness, charismatic. Christ's saying that "where two or three are gathered together in my name, there am I in the midst" must be understood in a new and radical way in our day of denominationalism and division within the church. He did not say "where two or three are gathered under this particular label (Baptist, Presbyterian, Pentecostal, etc.), there am I in the midst."

Coming Home

My experience of God's people who were of a completely different tradition than mine gave me pause for reflection. "Where," I had to ask myself, "is my identity? Am I an evangelical, a fundamentalist? What am I? Where do I belong?"

I remembered Paul's admonition to the Corinthian church: "For when one says, 'I belong to Paul,' and another, 'I belong to Apollos,' are you not merely men?" (1 Cor. 3:4).

Could it be, I asked, that we need to hear Paul's admonition today in a fresh way? Is the situation in today's church an expanded version of the Corinthian problem? Are we putting our labels before Christ? I was convinced that I had done this and I was resolved to find a way to overcome my failure to affirm the whole church. But I ran into trouble.

I began to declare this new-found sensitivity to the whole church to my classes at seminary and later to my students at Wheaton College. In those days, contrary to today, I found a considerable amount of resistance to my inclusive understanding of the church. Students and colleagues who hadn't shared my experience branded me as a papist, a Protestant going in the wrong direction, a betrayer of the true Protestant tradition. But I was resolved to maintain my convictions, which were born out of experience.

I was also desperate for fellowship with a community of people with whom my experience of a Christian identity, both Catholic and Protestant, was acceptable. I began to toss around the options in my mind. "Where should I go," I wondered. "Could I fit into the Lutheran church? Would I feel more at home in the Episcopal church?"

In an earlier chapter, I described my encounter with Leanne Payne who prayed for me in my office. For more than an hour Leanne prayed for me as I brought back to mind the wounds I had received by those who attempted to malign my faith pilgrimage and by those who sought to impede my journey into a wider, more inclusive sense of the Christian faith. After prayer, I felt free, even delivered. What other people thought, what other people said, what other people accused me of doing or believing no longer mattered. What was important for me was to pursue the direction in which I was being led.

Please don't feel that I am urging all others to follow my pilgrimage. I'm only explaining what happened to me. Part of the reason I ended up in the Episcopal church is that they consciously embraced both Catholic and Protestant traditions. That was more than ten years ago. A lot has happened in the church since then. One thing is the increasing openness to the Catholic tradition among Protestants. Many who would have been condemnatory of my pilgrimage in the early '70s are now much more open and accepting, because old prejudices have been in the process of breaking down in recent years. A new openness toward Protestants on the part of Catholics, and vice versa, has caused us to understand that there is only one church and that the label is secondary. I am a Christian first and an evangelical Episcopalian second.

God saves us not because of the label we wear, but because of what he has done in Jesus Christ for us all. When we truly affirm that confession, then we have found our identity with the history of all God's people. Our family tree begins not with the Reformation or the twentieth-century evangelical movement but with Jesus Christ, and it continues through the Apostles, the primitive Christian community, the Apostolic Fathers, the Eastern Orthodox Church, the Catholic Church, the Church of the Reformation, and all who say "Jesus is Lord."

* * *

To affirm our identity with all God's people everywhere is to recover from historical amnesia and to discover our identity. We belong to a great company of saints. We can claim Augustine, Aquinas, Luther, Calvin, Wesley, and Moody as our ancestors. We belong to them and they to us. Together we are one in Jesus Christ, brothers and sisters in the community of faith with Christ as our head. Thanks be to God!

5.

Embracing the Whole Church

———————————◆———————————

I find the best way for me to be an evangelical is to be an Episcopalian.

Bill Hill
Assistant Dean of Students
Wheaton College Graduate School

In addition to my teaching responsibilities at Wheaton College, I'm also an adjunct professor at Northern Baptist Seminary in Oak Brook, Illinois, a suburb of Chicago. I normally teach one course a year on early and medieval Christianity.

In the spring of 1983 I asked the students of my class to introduce themselves and tell a little about their background and hopes for the future.

One of the first students to speak began by saying, "Well, I grew up in the Catholic church. When I met the Lord, I left and became a Baptist." In this particular course there were at least four or five students out of twenty-two who recited a similar story, so, when it came time for me to give my story, I said, "Well, I grew up in a Baptist background, and when I met the Lord, I became an Episcopalian."

My comment was made tongue-in-cheek and I suspect that the others were as well. While the experience of leaving the Catholic church for these students may have been true, I didn't sense from them a judgmental attitude toward Catholics.

Nevertheless, many Protestants feel the Catholic church is so far removed from the true Christian tradition that those who are in it are not truly Christian. Only recently I was speaking to a Protestant who was telling me about his work in Latin America. As he described the area in which he worked, he said, "Of course there were no Christians there at all, they were all Catholics." I didn't feel it was my place to challenge or embarrass him in the presence of other people. I simply swallowed hard. I realized then and there that the attitude against Catholicism will die hard among Protestants.

But the opposite is true as well. A few years ago I taught a course at the Maryknoll Seminary (Roman Catholic) in Glen Ellyn, Illinois, on contemporary Protestantism. We began the course by swapping stories about our attitudes toward each other. Each of those seminarians confessed that they had grown up with the idea that Protestantism was a heresy, that they should stay away from Protestants, and that the likelihood of Protestants going to heaven was quite slim.

Barriers

Since the days of Vatican II, the barriers between Protestants and Catholics have been breaking down. However, we still have a long way to go before we truly recognize each other. Several recent examples from my own life seem to confirm this.

A few years ago my neighbor, a devout Roman Catholic woman, died. Her children came to me immediately after her death and told me that she had requested before she died that I preach her funeral sermon. Would I do it, I was asked. Of course I would do so, I replied. Shortly after, the priest of the local Catholic church called me to discuss the arrangements. He seemed very nervous and concerned about having a Protestant preach in the Catholic church. He told me that this was unusual, that it was not really allowed, but that since Mrs. Spratt had made the request, he would honor it. And, of course, he reminded me that I could not receive the Eucharist. Although I was aware that I could not receive the Eucharist, it still pained me to be shut out of the communion of those who also affirm Christ as Savior.

I preached on the phrase, "I am the resurrection and the life, he that believeth in me though he were dead, yet shall he live." I spoke of Mrs. Spratt's faith in Christ and her devotion to the church. I affirmed that as Jesus had actually been raised from the dead, so we who believe in him would be raised to everlasting life together with him and all the saints.

The orthodoxy of my sermon apparently caught the priest off-guard. He was an older man who probably still had strong misconceptions about Protestants. At the reception he seemed warmer toward me. He thanked me profusely for my sermon and registered surprise at my orthodoxy. I left with a strong feeling of unity and spiritual camaraderie between us.

A similar situation occurred recently in a Russian Orthodox church. Several years ago I taught a course in Eastern Orthodox theology at the Wheaton College summer school session. On one Sunday I scheduled a trip into Chicago to the Orthodox Cathedral, the Church of the Holy Trinity. The people at the church willingly cooperated with me. In addition to letting us attend their service, they appointed a woman who was very knowledgeable about Orthodoxy to meet with us and answer questions.

This woman was talking privately to several of my students. Convinced of her own faith and curious about these students from Wheaton College, she asked them "Who do you believe Jesus to be?" I suspect she thought they would say something like "a good man who left us an example to live by." Instead they said, "We believe he's the Son of God, who lived and died to redeem the world." The woman was aghast. "You don't say!" she exclaimed. "Why, you're orthodox." She immediately walked over to me and related the incident with a great deal of enthusiasm and amazement. Then, looking me in the eye, she asked, "Do any of these other students believe that?" "Yes," I said, "I can't speak for each one of them, but that certainly is what we believe and teach at Wheaton College." "My stars," she replied, "I didn't think anyone but the Orthodox and Catholics believed that."

I have told you these stories because they illustrate how isolated we are from one another and how suspicious we are of other Christians who are not from our immediate culture and context. Part of my reason for making a pilgrimage into the Episcopal church is it provides a context in which I can freely affirm the faith of other Christian people without being suspect. Let me share with you more of my background so you can understand why being able to make this broader affirmation of faith is a drawing card to the Episcopal church.

Separationism

I was first introduced to the theology of separationism while I was in junior high school. My father's experience as a pastor helped create within me the feeling that only those church groups that had left the major denominations were true churches standing in apostolic teaching.

In spite of my background I wasn't prepared for my introduction into "second-degree separationism" which I first experienced in my undergraduate days.

I'll never forget the day I heard the accusation that "Billy Graham is the greatest tool of the devil in the twentieth century." My mind flashed back to the day in high school when I first heard of Billy Graham. It was right after his Los Angeles crusade, which propelled him into the American limelight. I recalled how I read of him in *Life* magazine and looked at the pictures of his crusade as I sat in the library of the Lansdale High School in Pennsylvania. I remembered how excited I was to realize that someone who preached the gospel could also be accepted and even promoted by the media. I felt a spokesperson for me and others like myself, who were the despised believers of the world, had emerged.

The argument against Billy Graham was that he was flirting with modernism and compromising the gospel through his "co-operative evangelism." As an eighteen-year-old college student, I didn't have the wisdom nor the experience to deal with these assertions. But deep down within myself I could not believe what I was hearing. Yet, in the years to come I was to hear many others say the same thing. I was always troubled by second-degree separationism which taught that "true" Christians must not only separate from the liberals of the main line church but also from those evangelicals like Billy Graham who were compromising the true church by their association with these apostate ministers.

Why, I wondered, were we always so busy defining the perimeters in which truth and a right relationship to God were accurately defined? Was it really possible, I wondered, to have a pure church? The more I thought about this the more I felt that to be truly pure was an impossibility. The sheer logic of it creates split after split and an arrogance on the part of the splinter toward those who choose to remain. How can anyone except God himself be pure and uncontaminated from false belief, ethical error, and incomplete judgment? For me the so-called concept of the purity of the church was a strait-jacket that made me increasingly uncomfortable. It stifled my experience of the whole church and made me an outsider to the church through the ages.

The Ecumenical Movement

I was a graduate student at Concordia Theological Seminary between 1965 and 1968. And it was here that I took my first course in the ecumenical movement. I still remember the tension I experienced as I faced some of the issues about the unity of the Church of Jesus Christ.

Jesus' prayer in John 17, when he prayed "they may be one," impressed me and I have often referred to that prayer. Once, an evangelical who is strongly opposed to the concern for the unity of the church responded to my quotation of John 17 with the words "But that is only mentioned once in Scripture." I reminded him that the phrase "Ye must be born again" is also mentioned only once, but we have built a whole Christian tradition around it.

I was also impressed with the emphasis given to the unity of the church by the early church fathers. Clement of Rome, writing to the Christians of Corinth about a split in their church, said, "Why do we divide and tear to pieces the members of Christ, and raise up such strife against our own body . . . as to forget that we are members of one another?" Ignatius, Cyprian, Augustine, and others who wrote about the church expressed a similar concern. Cyprian, for example, saw the church as the "seamless robe" of Christ and illustrated how we could see the unity of the church as coming from its source. He reminded his readers that though there were many rivers there was only one source of water, and though there were many rays of the sun there was only one source of light. Another favorite image of the church is captured by Irenaeus, a second-century writer, in his statement, "The church . . . although scattered throughout the whole world . . . believes just as if she had one soul and one and the same heart." These words compelled me to examine my separatist attitude and to think about the church in a more global sense. I began to see more clearly the tragedy of the Reformation and longed for a reversal of those attitudes that separated me from my brothers and sisters in other denominations and expressions of the faith.

As I studied modern history, I saw how natural it was after the Reformation to harden the lines between groups of Christian people. I noticed, for example, that churches became set in their patterns and that a unity between certain denominations and a national identity was established. It seemed to me that Catholics were Italian and Polish, that Lutherans were German and Scandanavian, that the English were Anglican, and that the Scotts were Presbyterian. Free churches and new denominations emerged in all of these countries as they broke away from the state church under the conviction of separation of the church from secular control.

Gradually the various groups broke communication with one another and sought independence. They came to America to set up their distinct denominations, with their individual institutions and agencies, with very little cooperation or spirit of unity among them.

I was particularly interested to discover that the initial impulse toward ecumenicalism occurred on the mission field among evangelical Christians. Here, people from Anglican, Baptist, Lutheran, Methodist, and other traditions were working in competition with one another for the conversion of the same people. The absurdity of the situation was met with an attempt to unify the activities of the missionaries. This effort gradually grew into the present-day ecumenical movement.

It is true that the liberal element in the Protestant church took over the ecumenical movement in the middle of this century. As evangelicals broke away from main line denominations starting in the 1920s, they carried with them a perception that the ecumenical movement was something that was not only liberal but also dangerous and to be avoided.

In recent years many evangelicals have acknowledged that a significant shift away from a liberal theology toward apostolic Christianity has been occurring within the halls of the World Council of Churches and the National Council of Churches.

Evangelicals like Dr. Richard Lovelace, professor of church history at Gordon-Conwell Theological Seminary in Massachusetts and leader in the Council on Christian Union, are giving Evangelicals a new voice in ecumenical circles. In a recent interview with Dr. Lovelace, he said, "When I was a seminarian at Westminister I kept asking myself, 'What's the right denomination?' and the only answer I could get out of Scripture was that there is no right denomination. They're all wrong. The whole system is wrong."

My own model of an ecumenical spirit in the twentieth century is Billy Graham. Dr. Graham exhibits a spirit of love toward Christians of all sorts. He has worked with every Protestant denomination; he has made friends in the Orthodox church as well as in the Catholic church. He has moved with great spiritual agility within all these traditions.

I think we must ask why Dr. Graham has been able to demonstrate an ecumenical spirit and embrace these traditions and have members of the various traditions embrace him in return.

I believe it comes down to the fact that Dr. Graham is concerned about preaching the gospel of Jesus Christ without getting caught up in the trappings of culture and national identity that each denomination carries. He is able to accent the trans-

cultural aspect of the gospel that one finds in every believing
tradition. The simple fact is that when we peel away the secondary layers of tradition, we are able to get back to the apostolic
interpretation given to the Christ-event.

My problem with those who fight against the unity of the
church is that they often do so on the grounds of secondary
issues. We may not all agree that the Bible is inerrant, but we
can agree that it is the authoritative apostolic witness to Jesus
Christ. We may not be able to agree on our specific interpretation of bread and wine, but we can at least agree that they are
the symbols of Christ living, dying, and rising again for our
salvation. We may not be able to agree on our specific interpretation and practice of baptism, but we ought to be able to agree
that this is God's sign to us of his grace and love toward us. We
may not be able to agree on the specifics of the end times, but
we can agree on the coming again of Christ.

* * *

In the Episcopal church I find a healthy sense of unity and
diversity. In this tradition we recognize that that which holds the
church together is more important than that which divides the
church.

I like to view the church as a house that is built upon certain
pillars. Its pillars include the Scripture, the early creeds, the
sacraments, the order of oversight, ministry and service, worship, and a responsibility for the life of the world. Although
there may be diversity within these areas, we are united in matters of faith.

My choice is to stress this unity and acknowledge our differences as the human and cultural element of the church. I want to
both affirm all God's people everywhere and seek to understand,
affirm, and enjoy the differences between us. I can do this in the
Episcopal church.

6.

Growing into a Holistic Spirituality

In the Anglican tradition, I have found a profound experience of spirituality that takes me out of my daily life, puts me in the presence of God, then returns me to my daily life with a renewed heart and life. And I don't feel that I'm out there alone, unconnected, unrelated, uninfluenced by what has gone before me. I'm part of a broad Christian tradition.

Walter Elwell
Professor of Theology
Wheaton Graduate School

In the fall of 1983 Bishop Jon Braun of the Evangelical Orthodox Church wrote and told me he was coming through Wheaton. "Could we get together?" he asked. I not only wanted to get
together with him, I wanted him to talk to my class about his
pilgrimage into Orthodoxy because we were studying the Orthodox church at that time.

In the course of his lecture he made a comment that has stuck
with me. I want to share it with you. He was speaking about his
upbringing in a Christian home and the fact that as a young
person he had always believed but had had no dramatic experience of salvation. His parents, anxious for him to have a dramatic conversion experience, began to push him toward a decision. "This," he said soberly, "actually pushed me out of the
church and made me think for a temporary period of time that I
was an unbeliever." He then went on to say that placing too
much emphasis on a dateable experience of salvation can be
dangerous if we do not take into account that many who grow
up in Christian homes grow into faith without such an experience. When they are forced toward a decision they have already
made quietly, they may begin to think of themselves as unbeliev-
ers.

This illustration points to the tension between the spirituality
of justification and sanctification. Both aspects of believing in
Christ and growing in Christ are complementary to each other.

A Spirituality of Conversion

Evangelicals are strong in the spirituality of conversion. Evangelical history is in itself a history of those spurts of revival that
have dotted the church through the ages. We stand in the tradition of Justin Martyr, Gregory of Nyssa, St. Francis of Assisi,
John Wycliffe, Martin Luther, John Wesley, Jonathan Edwards,
D.L. Moody, and many others who have experienced a dramatic
encounter with Jesus Christ.

Certainly, a dramatic experience of the saving reality of Christ
is not to be denied or minimized. Such an experience born of
God by the power of the Holy Spirit makes a powerful impact
on the personality and has the positive effect of making one see
life through new eyes. It is not unusual to find people leaving the
liturgical tradition because of its failure to stress conversion ade-

quately. On the other hand, it is not unusual to find evangelicals leaving evangelical churches because they overstress conversion and inadequately emphasize growth in Christ. Let me describe some of those approaches to spirituality within evangelicalism that some of us find inadequate.

A Spirituality of Dos and Don'ts

My first memory of a postconversion spirituality is what I call a spirituality of *dos* and *don'ts*. As far back as I can remember, the dos were: read your Bible every day, pray daily, witness to other people, stay away from evil haunts, keep yourself pure, and get involved in the local church. The don'ts were just as clear: don't smoke, dance, drink, go to the theatre, or play cards.

I am not totally against a spirituality of dos and don'ts. New Testament writers give evidence of a similar kind of spirituality among the early Christians. In Galatians 5, Paul states, "Do not walk after the flesh." Then he gives a list of those sins of the flesh that Christians should avoid. In the same passage he admonishes the Christian convert to "walk after the Spirit," after which he lists the fruits of the Spirit. Paul gives a similar negative and positive list in Colossians 3, where he admonishes new Christians to "put off the old man" and to "put on the new man." This same concept of a contrasting list of dos and don'ts is found in early Christian literature such as the *Didache* written around 100 A.D. Scholars recognize these lists as instructions surrounding baptism. It has been strongly suggested that memorizing lists that guide behavior and attempting to live by the rules implied within them may have a positive effect on Christian life.

What I and others like me find objectionable are the manmade rules that have grown out of the New Testament spirituality. When rules against smoking, drinking, and dancing are turned into absolutes, they cheapen true spirituality. They make spirituality too simple because they bypass the weightier matters such as concern for justice. The list is what Bonhoeffer called a cheap grace. It is a set of rules that is fairly *easy* to follow.

In my experience I have found that people often live by these rules because they feel pressured from the group that demands conformity, rather than committed from the heart. Let me give you an example. At Bob Jones University I was a "preacher boy." A preacher boy was any student who was planning to go into some form of ministry. All future Christian workers (male only) met once a week in the preacher boys' class and were given practical instruction on how to build a church, run a Sunday school, and things of that sort. In addition to our weekly meeting we were required to witness to seven people a week and hand in a report detailing our conversation and the results.

There were close to one thousand students in that class. If you multiply that by seven, it means that seven thousand witnesses a week for thirty-four weeks of the year were being made by preacher boys alone. That's two hundred and thirty-eight thousand contacts a year in the environs of Greenville, South Carolina!

Now, there were times that I was committed and I fulfilled the spirit of that expectation. I often went away for weekends to work in a local church and community. Frequently these jaunts proved very positive. However, there were other times, which were more frequent than I care to admit, when I had a paper or an exam pressing me. These times were characterized by a quick trip to Greenville with seven tracts. I would simply hand out the tract and say, "Are you saved?" hoping the person would not want to engage in a long conversation. I'd then hastily write up my report and turn it in to satisfy the requirement of being a witness.

To say that my conscience bothered me about this approach to witnessing is an understatement. I'm still sensitive about this kind of impersonal witness and uncomfortable with personal witnessing in general. Keeping the rule in this instance undermined the sheer joy of being a witness because I was acting under pressure rather than from the heart. Similar responses can be seen anytime the letter of the Law is pressed too far.

A Spirituality of Believing the Right Thing

In seminary and graduate school I encountered another kind of spirituality that I will call an intellectual spirituality of believing the right doctrine. Again, like the spirituality of dos and don'ts there is a biblical basis to the spirituality of correct doctrine. This kind of spirituality is found in the writings of Paul, especially when he admonishes the early Christians not to follow after the heresies that were already arising in the first century. In the Pastoral Epistles, in Colossians, and in other passages, he urges Christians to stand fast in the truth that has been handed down from the apostles.

For example, in 1 Corinthians 15, Paul is battling with a faction in the church that is denying the bodily resurrection of Jesus from the dead. He appeals to these people to hold fast to the tradition of truth he handed over to them. Then he reminds his readers about the message he delivered to them: "For I delivered to you as of first importance what I also received, that Christ died for our sins in accordance with the scriptures, that he was buried, that he was raised on the third day in accordance with the scriptures" (vv. 3–4).

I think it is generally agreed that the content of the Apostles' Creed represents an essential summary of apostolic Christianity. Early Christians learned this creed in preparation for baptism; and when they were baptized, they were not only baptized in the name of the Father, Son, and Holy Spirit, but also in the simple truths about the Triune God proclaimed in the Apostles' Creed. (The earliest form of this creed is called the Interrogatory Creed and can be found in *The Apostolic Tradition* written about 220 A.D.)

But the kind of spirituality of right doctrine to which I refer goes beyond the basic affirmation of faith and into a particular and precise interpretation of the faith. Let me give you an example of what I mean. Recently I was a guest speaker at a church in the Midwest. The people in this particular congregation very consciously adhere to strict Calvinism, especially on the issue of the sovereignty of God, the question of election, and God's providence. Before I spoke, I had dinner with several of the church's elders. During our conversation, I was asked a number of leading questions, which I could tell were tests of my spiritual orthodoxy. Although the people were most kind and gracious, these questions made me uncomfortable. I didn't feel that I was being accepted for my faith in Christ. Rather, I felt as if I was being examined for my adherence to a particular system of interpreting Christ. I thought my answers were not totally acceptable. And I began to feel like an outsider rather than a welcomed member of the group.

One tragic aspect of the spirituality of right doctrine is that it tends to create a uniformity of interpretation which stifles growth. Recently, I was talking to a student who transferred to Wheaton College from a fundamentalist college. I asked him, "Tony, how does Wheaton differ from your other educational experience?"

"Well, to tell you the truth, it's a breath of fresh air," he said.

"How so?" I responded with curiosity.

"I'm allowed to think here."

"What do you mean?" I asked, my curiosity growing by the second.

"In my Bible classes at the other college I began to question some of the interpretations of the institution. I simply wanted answers to some very honest questions about why we believe and practice certain things. The answers I was getting were not satisfactory. So I pushed harder."

"You challenged the professor?"

"Right. I don't think I was obnoxious about it. But apparently the teacher felt the questions were evidence that I was falling away from the truth."

"Why, what happened?"

"He called me into his office for a special session."

"Yes."

"He said, 'Tony, I'm really worried about you. You seem to be slipping spiritually. I'd like to have prayer with you and ask God to get hold of your life again.' "

"And how did you interpret that?"

"It was obvious to me and clear from our conversation that questioning was unacceptable. What is truly spiritual is believing what you are told. A questioning spirit is a doubting spirit and a doubting spirit comes from an unbelieving heart. That's what it boils down to."

Unfortunately this kind of conversation could be repeated thousands of times. The mentality of the spirituality of right belief can become, as it did for Tony, a stifling experience of not being able to show some healthy doubt about the faith or its particular denominational interpretation. It is not uncommon for doubters to learn how to keep their mouth shut to keep out of trouble. The tragedy of this approach to spirituality is that it leads to a mouthing of the faith that lacks integrity.

In the Anglican tradition I have found a freedom of curiosity and openness. I regularly speak in Episcopal churches where, during the discussion, a considerable number of viewpoints will be expressed openly and forcefully. I've found a give and take on the local parish level that is healthy and dynamic.

An Ethical Spirituality

In the late '60s and early '70s I first encountered what I will call an ethical spirituality. I speak particularly of the spirituality that is concerned for the poor, the oppressed, and the downtrodden.

Certainly ethical spirituality is a strong and even central motif in the life and teachings of Jesus. His mission was chiefly to the poor, to the outcasts of society.

In the late '60s, the civil rights movement and opposition to the war in Vietnam, together with an exposure to economic injustice in this country and political imperialism around the world, caused many an evangelical's consciousness to be raised.

Jim Wallis, the editor of *Sojourners,* was a student at that time at Trinity Seminary in Deerfield, Illinois. John Alexander, the editor of *The Other Side,* was teaching philosophy at Wheaton College. Both of these young men were friends of mine and they began to expand my conscience and sense of Christian ethical responsibility.

In the fall of 1973, Jim Wallis and John Alexander, together with Ron Sider and others, organized a number of evangelicals to meet at the old Y.M.C.A. building in Chicago to discuss the evangelical conscience in the face of growing national and world-wide issues of ethical importance. Out of that conference came the historic Chicago Declaration, a forthright call to Evangelicals to embrace an ethical spirituality.

All of us at the conference were organized into various groups for discussion. I was assigned to the economic responsibility group. I remember how appalled I was at the discussion. The issue at stake was the meaning of Jesus' words, "Take up your cross and follow after me." The specific question under debate was. "Could one be rich and be a Christian?" The word "rich" was never really defined then so it is difficult for me now to state categorically what was meant by the term. But one of the members of the group was a man very interested in social issues. He also happened to be a successful businessman. He shared with us that his salary was over $100,000 a year, that he drove a Mercedes-Benz, and that he owned a small yacht. Could he qualify as a Christian? His question was sincere. Finally we went around the circle and each person responded to the gentleman's question. The consensus was that if he really wanted to follow after Jesus, he would need to give up his job, sell his belongings, and give the proceeds to the poor. Then he would be in a position to follow after Christ.

I firmly believe in ethical spirituality, but in this case I felt it was carried too far. Like the other kinds of spirituality I had encountered in my pilgrimage, ethical spirituality was being turned into something legalistic and wooden. It was coming from the outside asking for a legal conformity to a set of man-made rules.

I do not judge Jim Wallis, John Alexander, or Ron Sider. Although they have taken personal vows to live on a poverty level, I don't feel that they negatively judge others who have not chosen to follow an ethical spirituality to this degree. What I am concerned about is the legalistic interpretation that others have made from this life-style choice.

A Spirituality of Experience

More recently I have come into contact with what I will call the spirituality of experience in the Anglican tradition. I and others like myself are increasingly attracted to this particular form of spirituality. It is not a substitute for the other spiritualities I have described. Rather, it is complementary to them and contains them all in its larger orbit.

I can best define the spirituality of experience by describing it as the attempt to integrate Christ with all of life. Let me describe three forms of this spiritual experience that have attracted me toward the Episcopal spiritual tradition.

It was in the context of the Episcopal church that I first heard of the Jesus prayer. Although the Jesus prayer is primarily an Eastern Orthodox form of spirituality, it has also been accepted in the West by Catholics and Anglicans. The Jesus prayer is the simple prayer "Lord Jesus Christ, Son of God, have mercy on me a sinner."

The prayer originates from the attitude of the penitent sinner who prayed, "Lord, have mercy on me a sinner," a prayer that becomes clearer when contrasted to the prayer of the Pharisee who said, "Lord, I thank thee that I am not as these others, publicans and sinners."

It is a prayer of the heart, an attitude prayer that gained prominence as a lay devotion in the Eastern Church. It has some similarities to Brother Andrew's "practicing the presence of God."

The prayer is to be repeated again and again as a means of establishing a continuing relationship with God. It is short enough to be said with the beat of the heart. To this day, people who use this form of prayer will sometimes rest their chin on their chest and allow their eyes to gaze on the area of the heart as a symbol of uniting both head and heart and thus the whole person in the prayer.

The content of the prayer is thoroughly evangelical. It affirms the full title of Christ, acknowledges our sin, and assures us of his mercy. I often find myself saying this prayer as I walk or drive or as I lie down to sleep. I feel the presence of Christ through this prayer—a unity with him and his saving action for me.

Another thoroughly Christ-centered spirituality that attracts me to the Anglican tradition is what has been called Eucharistic spirituality. This is a spirituality born of the conviction that the Eucharist represents the saving action of Christ at work. I have already referred to a supernatural understanding of the Eucharist in the Anglican tradition, a prerequisite, I believe, for the experience of Eucharistic spirituality.

Eucharistic spirituality is the experience of being spiritually nourished and strengthened by eating the bread and drinking the wine. Since I perceive this as God doing something for me, I find myself drawn to the Eucharist as a necessary part of my spiritual diet. The mystery of what Christ did for me on the cross reaches into my inner person in a way that I cannot describe.

John Calvin described the Eucharist as a "sign," a "pledge," a "testimony" of God's work on our behalf. These are nouns that imply an action. I can now understand these terms of Calvin, not because I have intellectualized them, but because I have experienced internally the power of Christ's action for me.

In the Eucharist I feel both saved again and compelled to live in the Eucharistic way. Both justification and sanctification are communicated to me. Bread and wine speaks to me of my sin. But it at once communicates the saving reality of Christ. I am caught up in its power and cleansed by the fresh work of the Holy Spirit which I continually experience at that Table of Communion.

A third spirituality of experience is the discipline of following the church year as a personal devotion. I've always had a difficult time maintaining a continuous devotion in my life. Like others, I've probably tried everything in the book.

The church year is a schedule for living through the life of Christ in a systematic way. It begins with Advent, when Scripture readings and the corporate life of the church begin to center on the coming birth of Christ. During this time, my life is directed toward a more spiritual experience of Christmas because I am called upon both individually and within the corporate worshiping community to center on the coming of Christ. During Christmas, which lasts for twelve days not just one, I am led into a fuller experience of the babe born in Bethlehem. And during Epiphany, the season that celebrates the manifestation of Christ to the world, I am personally and corporately drawn into the witness of Christ and his church to the world.

The period from Advent to Epiphany drops off in intensity after January 6 until the beginning of Lent on Ash Wednesday. Lent begins a very intense period of personal spiritual examination, which leads toward renewal and deeper faith. Lent is a time to reflect deeply on my personal relationship to Christ. It is a different spiritual experience than that of Advent, Christmas, or Epiphany. During Lent I am called upon to enter into the sufferings of Jesus and to prepare for his death.

For me, this discipline has made Holy Week and Easter an experience of spiritual vigor and joy that goes far beyond my old attitude of "Oops, here it is Easter, already." Preparation for Easter that takes me into the tomb has given me a much more vital spiritual participation in the resurrection of Christ and a deeper sense and experience of that resurrection joy which I celebrate individually and corporately until Pentecost. During Pentecost season, the emphasis shifts to the power of the Holy Spirit that brings the church into existence. I am called upon to receive the Holy Spirit's power anew and to engage myself in the study of the Epistles.

What I like most is the variety in spiritual experience that is given to me in the discipline of the following church year. Further, the fact that the whole church is celebrating the same events provides a leadership in spirituality that is outside of my own meager efforts. I join with other pilgrims in the faith as together we reenact the significant moments in the life of Christ that draw us into unity with him and with his purpose.

* * *

I find when most people are honest about their spiritual pilgrimage, they admit to the difficulty of maintaining the habit of a spiritual discipline. What attracts me most about the Anglican spiritual tradition is that it provides purposeful spiritual direction into the life of Christ. And I am not alone. Others are walking the same path with me, assisting me on my way, helping me when I fail, encouraging me in the journey we are taking together. Therefore, I have asked several of these evangelicals on the Canterbury Trail to tell about their experiences. In the next section of this book, six pilgrims will share their stories.

Six Pilgrims
Share Their Stories

7.

Michael Anderson

I read once about the odd eating habits of the boa constrictor. He swallows his prey whole, without chewing. If the catch is large enough, he is unable to move and he simply goes to sleep until it all digests.

My decision to join the Episcopal church was not primarily the result of a logical process, meticulously carried out to its inevitable end. I read and prayed and thought a good deal about the decision, but in the end I was drawn to the life and worship of the Anglican church from an inner longing, a soul-craving that the mind often strains to comprehend. When I finally met Anglicanism I seized upon it from an impulse of the heart. I swallowed it whole without chewing. That was seven years ago and I am still digesting my prey.

* * *

I grew up in a three-storied house on top of a hill in a small town in South Dakota. I was the second of seven children and thanks to my father's industry (he owned a small business) and my mother's frugality, we enjoyed a comfortable living.

We were a Christian family. My parents taught us by word

and act the supreme importance of knowing Jesus Christ as Savior. There was set before us all a vision of heroic Christianity,
which called for complete personal sacrifice in the pursuit of
holiness and the advancement of Christ's kingdom. I was born
again at the age of seven during a daily vacation Bible school
held one summer at the Baptist church where we were members.
We all went to church, Sunday school, and mid-week prayer
service faithfully, but the most significant formation in the faith
occurred at home.

On the walls there were plaques with Bible verses and religious sayings on them. One plaque, which hung near the telephone in the hallway, read:

> Only one life 'twill soon be past;
> Only what's done for Christ will last.

Reverential pictures also decorated the walls. There was one of
the old, white-bearded man sitting at a rough table with head
bowed and hands folded over a loaf of bread. And there was one
of Jesus with the little children gathered around. I identified
with the little boy in the picture who stood there in his pleated
pants waiting to show the Lord his toy airplane.

It was our custom to have family devotions. This was irregular
at first, but the longer we worked at it, the more consistent it
became. We cleared the table after the evening meal and we
would all fetch our Bibles. I do not remember that we went
through the Bible with any pattern, nor were there any long
explanations of the readings. My mother, especially, trusted the
Bible to speak for itself.

After this we would all kneel beside our chairs. If time permit-
ted, and it usually did, we prayed "all around." I remember
enjoying the quiet and the peace. When sometimes the prayers
seemed to last too long, I distracted myself by staring at the
vinyl seat of my chair, making little craters with my elbows and
watching them disappear. We would often sing after the prayers,
while we still knelt. I loved this most of all. We avoided the
giddy choruses we learned at Sunday school, singing instead the
more reverent hymns such as "When I Survey the Wondrous
Cross." There was one chorus which was a special favorite of my

mother. It had a serene and haunting melody and we would sing
it slowly and very quietly:

Worthy is the Lord and mighty is his name;
King of heav'n, yet down to earth he came.
Angels sing his praise and I will do the same.
Worthy is the Lord, all glory to his name.

We waited in quietness after this, and more often than not my
mother got up from her knees wiping her eyes of tears.

I came to know, in these family devotions, a God, awesome
and majestic, who was not to be approached lightly, with the
familiarity that so often characterized evangelical worship. I recognized a discrepancy between our family worship and the worship of the church. At home we obeyed our instincts. The kneeling, the quietness, and the low singing seemed an appropriate
response to the dark majesty of Almighty God.

It was different at church. The services were usually ebullient
and excessively cheery. The lights were bright. We never knelt,
of course, and we seemed unsettled by silence. All the spaces
were filled up with talking or singing and organ preludes, post-
ludes, and interludes. This was especially hard on my mother.
Sometimes, when the special music was particularly bad (we
occasionally had to endure saxophone solos), she would give out
a muffled sigh and bow her head. Although I couldn't know it at
the time, these services, week after week, would stir in me a
search for a satisfying worship, a worship worthy of the God we
knew.

This is why, perhaps, I was so taken with the activities of Dr.
and Mrs. Dilger who lived next door. The Dilgers were Roman
Catholics and our yards, as if by design, were separated by a
great, long hedge. Virtually every morning the doctor (he was a
dentist) and his wife would leave the house and walk down the
hill for the 6:30 mass. I was baffled by this dedication, but I was
bound to regard it as a ritual of questionable value.

I did not trust the doctor. He was hunchbacked, which made
him walk with a crooked gait. He was also known to drill out
cavities without Novocaine. Mrs. Dilger, on the other hand, was
a kindly old woman who seemed, above all, to be at peace with

herself and the world. If we were certain that the Catholics were
pitifully deceived and hopelessly lost, we were willing to make
an exception for Mrs. Dilger. She widened our categories.

The Dilger house was strange. I recall being at once shocked
and enchanted by the enormous number of images that seemed
to occupy virtually every empty corner, especially the seat of the
big bay window in the hall near the parlor. Among the gerani-
ums were dozens of plastic saints, which jarred both my religious and aesthetic sensibilities. Outside on the front lawn stood
a life-size statue of the Virgin Mary ensconced in a stone grotto
which the doctor had built. One day, for no apparent reason, he
began to build the shrine and our family watched through the
hedge as the old hunchback transformed piles of sand, stones,
gravel, and cement into a shelter for the Blessed Virgin. It never
occurred to us to consider this a labor of love. We thought of it,
rather, as a work of supererogation that devout Catholics occasionally felt required to perform.

Once when I was sent next door just before supper to borrow
some eggs, I knocked on the screen door and found myself
square in the middle of the "Daily Family Rosary," which was
being broadcast over the local radio station. The doctor and his
family were kneeling in the kitchen and someone waved me in to
join them. I knelt down (this is what we did at home), and
before long I heard myself repeating the Our Fathers and Hail
Marys right along with the rest. I was amazed at how easily
these Catholic prayers fell off my lips and I marvelled at the
earnestness with which Mrs. Dilger fingered her beads. Later
that evening, on the other side of the hedge, as I knelt at our
table, I couldn't help noting the similarity of devotion. They had
their ritual; we had ours.

At some point in those early years I began to feel the call into
"full-time Christian service." I do not remember when it first
came, but it was a feeling that grew and did not go away. After
high school, I enrolled in the Prairie Bible Institute to prepare
myself for this vocation. The Prairie Bible Institute was a four-
year missionary-training school situated on the flat wheatfields
of southern Alberta in Canada. The school's motto was "Training Disciplined Soldiers for Christ," and the martial ethos was
evident everywhere. Like the surrounding prairies, the campus
was austere, and the smallest details of our personal lives were

regulated by rules or bells. It was a bit like a Protestant monastery. Everything was designed to turn one's attention from the distractions of common life to the more serious business of learning the Bible. This we undertook with boot-camp zeal. It was a good and healthy experience for me, and apart from some glaring eccentricities and a certain narrowness of vision, the school tutored me in a rather moderate form of fundamentalism. I was much moved by the teaching and preaching of the founder and president, L. E. Maxwell, whose emphasis on balance and breadth kept the Institute from skidding off into extremes. I can pay the man no higher tribute—he has since passed away—than to say that he made me love and revere Holy Scripture.

It would be hard to establish the theological pedigree of the Institute. It was preeminently a product of the rise of American Fundamentalism in the early years of this century. It has a strong Anabaptist strain, moderated by a mild Calvinism and the English Keswick movement. But the Institute did not think in terms of theological or denominational alignment. The Bible, it was felt, spoke literally and unambiguously on all the major issues of faith and practice and therefore church history, traditions, councils, and creeds had negligible value for the common Christian. Quite by accident I discovered a book that challenged that assumption.

One day while browsing in the Institute's book store, I picked up a copy of F. F. Bruce's *Tradition: Old and New.* Here was a book, written by someone who was considered a "safe" evangelical. But its central thesis was that every denomination, in its doctrine, worship, and customs, was in enormous debt to the ancient church as it had developed through the centuries. It also claimed that this was true even in those circles where this debt was most vigorously denied. The idea fascinated me.

Within this book I encountered strange-sounding names: Irenaeus, Tertullian, Cyprian. Was I, a simple Christian in the barracks of fundamentalism, heir to these men? It seemed I was. But what then could this mean? What would happen if I began to read the history of the church seriously, if I allowed my settled views of the Bible, of theology, of the church to be tempered and informed by these men and others like them? I had learned earlier to ignore them merely because they were ancients or, more to the point, because they were inclined to say things we were simply not prepared to hear: things "catholic," things "sacramental." I felt like Josiah discovering the lost books of the Law in the walls of the temple. And like the king, I found myself thrust abruptly into the disturbing light of this vast section of my religious heritage, an area to which I had been, for so many years, shamefully oblivious.

Far from being at the doorstep of Canterbury, however, I was still quite comfortable in my present tradition. I was not aware that these ideas were carrying me anywhere at all; I knew only the euphoria of finding them. And so my years at the Institute were characterized by an odd harmony of ideas—familiar melodies played off in counterpoint against these more novel themes.

Our tradition, for example, effectively denied the notion of sacrament—that material things could be instruments of grace, vehicles of the Divine. The divorce of matter and spirit had been granted on grounds of mutual incompatibility. Of course we talked about the doctrines of Creation and Incarnation. We even discussed Gnosticism and the metaphysical dualism that was its foundation. But still we harbored a basic distrust of the earth and the things of the earth, even our own humanity. (It never occurred to us that the path of this suspicion, if we followed it all the way out, might just lead us into gnostic territory.) Ours was a spiritual religion whose text was the dictum of Christ: "God is spirit, and those who worship him must worship in spirit and truth" (John 4:24).

I remember noting a certain inconsistency between this doctrine and our observance of the two ordinances, baptism and the Lord's Supper. I was on a date (with the woman who would eventually become my wife) and I remember telling her how odd these ceremonies had appeared to me lately. All the fuss of baptism—the tank of water, the white robe, the kerchief over the nose, and the indelicate dunking of the candidate—suddenly seemed an irksome intrusion into our "spiritual" worship. Here was a peculiar irony, a Baptist chagrined by baptism.

And why, furthermore, were we required to bother with the elements of Holy Communion? I had been doing this all my life, but now it made no sense. Suddenly the bread and grape juice seemed an almost pagan contamination of things. Couldn't we just sit quietly and recall the Lord's death? I asked others these questions but always received the same reply: the Lord had required the ordinance. No one seemed to wonder why. It was a clear command of Scripture and that was what mattered.

But I could not believe that this ordinance was merely an arbitrary mandate. I had a vague sense that in the rite of Communion the church had received divinely inspired clues both to the nature of her redemption and of the whole created order. What I could not see then was that the worship of an incarnate God required a corresponding carnality; that as God had given himself to us, wrapped in flesh and blood, we would enclose our worship of him in bread and wine, in water, oil, fire, and smoke, with bodies bowed and knees bent. The Incarnation did not introduce a new principle. Rather, the Word made Flesh, the Sacrament of God, opened our eyes to see the sacramentality of all things, the coinherence of God and his world, every creature animated with the Creator's breath.

But I was a long way from articulating these replies; only the questions had been formed. So, while some of my friends upon graduating from the Institute were taking churches and going off to mission fields, I felt ill-prepared. I therefore applied to a large, nondenominational seminary in the States. But because it required an undergraduate degree, I first began looking at colleges.

About this time I discovered Thomas Howard's autobiography, *Christ the Tiger*. It was the story of a young man who had, it seemed, gone through many of the struggles I now was going through. In addition, it was witty, robust, and urbane. I put the book down with a sigh, thinking that the one book I might ever be inclined to write had already been written. I was intrigued to learn that he was both an Episcopalian and an alumnus of Wheaton College in Illinois. I decided to continue my education at Wheaton.

My fiancée and I were married a month before the fall term began and I took a job as choir director at a Baptist church in a town about twenty miles from the college. After sampling the courses, I decided to major in English literature. I was greatly influenced by the poetry of the seventeenth-century metaphysicals, especially Donne and Herbert. I didn't take many courses in the Bible department since I had just left one "seminary" and was on my way to another, but I did elect one course in the history of theology that turned out to be one more nudge along the Canterbury Trail.

One afternoon the professor was discussing the Reformation, diagramming the movement on the chalkboard. He delineated some of the major branches of Protestant tradition, then some of the off-shoots of these traditions, and off-shoots of these off-shoots, and so on. Here was the Big Bang in the sixteenth century from which the modern theological universe had burst forth. I was fascinated. I was also dismayed for I located my tradition, the Anabaptist, among those which had to be described as remotely separated. I was disoriented; it was a Copernican revolution and I found myself floating on the fringes of the galaxy not only with respect to Rome, but also to the bulk of Protestantism. Instinctively I began to doubt the validity of that position. I felt the burden of proof shift onto my shoulders. It seemed to me that anyone in this position of extreme separation was required to declare why he remained there. I determined to begin doing that. Thankfully, help was close at hand.

This same professor, as an adjunct to his courses, often took students on field trips to a variety of churches, including his own, a small Episcopal parish near the college which had become a kind of asylum for Wheaton students and faculty for whom standard evangelicalism had begun to wear thin. This was my first taste of the Episcopal church, my first exposure to formal liturgy. The rich, reverent worship, the grand music, and the experience of sharing the Eucharist with friends and strangers who loved a common Lord moved me profoundly. Because I was working in the Baptist church, I could not regularly attend services at this parish, but I had seen and heard and felt things there that I knew I could never forget.

Gradually I began to feel that my decision to attend the non-denominational seminary had been premature. I still felt called to the ministry, but I was discovering things in the world and in myself that made me wonder if I could really be satisfied in my present tradition. I was at an impasse and I graduated from Wheaton with no real strategy for the future. The Baptist church, in a generous response to my dilemma, offered to expand my responsibilities and pay me accordingly while I decided what to do next.

In this new capacity I began meeting with the pastoral staff and together we evaluated our worship service. We asked for more quiet before the services. I chose more and more music from the "Worship" and "Praise" sections of the hymnal. We introduced the Advent wreath and made a few modest attempts to follow the church year. At one point the choir was even singing the Psalms to a slightly modernized version of Gregorian chant—a tribute, I think, to a highly unusual Baptist church.

Many appreciated the changes, but there were others who felt that they represented a fundamental incongruity, as though something alien had crept in. Once, in a congregational meeting, a lady who remains a dear friend to this day, spoke her mind plainly: "I'm a Baptist," she said. "If I wanted to sit in silence before the service, chant the Psalms, and sing hymns in a minor key, I guess I'd become an Episcopalian or something." I remember nodding to myself: Yes, I suppose that's what a person might have to do.

There is, after all, a point beyond which no tradition ought to be stretched. Every group has its own integrity and it is a matter of decency, at least, not to violate the limits that define it. I had been trying to impose Anglican forms on a Baptist piety. It occurred to me that it might make more sense to take the opposite approach. The Anglican communion was certainly broad enough to encompass my evangelical spirit. Nothing I could bring to the church could possibly startle her; she already knew thousands like me.

One year later my wife and I left the Baptist church and began attending services at a little Episcopal parish in the same town. Soon after, we were confirmed. In the Cathedral of St. James in Chicago, I knelt before the bishop to receive the laying on of hands. The "Amen" at the end of his prayer was not merely the completion of the rite. For me it was also the last word in a long and twisted and complex sentence, which among other things had asked, "What form shall my faith take?"

Shortly after this I attended a conference at an old Anglo-Catholic parish in Chicago, sponsored by a group of Episcopalians who were concerned for renewal in the church. In the morning, Philip Edgcumbe Hughes lectured on the centrality of Holy Scripture in the church's life. Then Thomas Howard regaled us with stories of his childhood—growing up in a strict evangelical home, later becoming an Episcopalian, and finding to his amazement that the two experiences were remarkably compatible. The people responded with great buoyancy to both men.

At midday, we shared in a Solemn Pontifical High Mass. The celebrant, Bishop Atkins of Wisconsin, presided with unselfconscious dignity and grace. I still remember the billowing incense, the noonday light streaming in, and the joy with which the people and the organ sang together. I was transfixed. All I could think of was Isaiah's vision of God: "The foundations of the thresholds shook . . . and the house was filled with smoke" (Isaiah 6:4). It seemed that all of man's art and ingenuity and skill was being called upon to adore and extol Almighty God.

Something in my soul said yes to this. What I had felt as a child—kneeling for prayers at the dining room table, the strange attraction of Catholic devotion, my study of the Scripture, all this, and a young man's yearning to give himself to God without reserve—seemed to meet together there. I remember saying to myself, "This is it. I have come home. This is a vision that simply must not die."

After the conference in Chicago, we went back to our little stone church with plank pews and sagging, wooden floors. Here there were no dazzling liturgies, no splendor or spectacle, only the enduring sustenance, coming to the altar, week in and week out, to receive the bread of life. What struck me was the way in which this little church, like the big one downtown, was faithfully, simply lifting up Jesus Christ. It should not have surprised me for it is the nature of the Eucharist to do so. Music dies, colors fade, and incense drifts away, but the essence of it, what the Eucharist unfailingly does, whether in a mighty cathedral or a humble hall, is to exalt him. The mass is the vessel in which Christ is lifted up before the church, showing him to be all her life and hope, her glory and her final goal. This steady devotion to the Lord Christ in the sacrament of the altar, which is at the center of classic Anglican spirituality, is the thing that drew me and held me and holds me still.

It was perhaps inevitable that in this environment my interest in the ministry should flower again. I had found a home in the Episcopal church; now I wanted to minister in that church. My wife and I began to think about seminary training again, but in the five years since my graduation from college we had become entrenched in suburban life. We now had three children, we owned a home, and I was working for a local newspaper. I needed to go to school but there seemed to be no visible means whereby we could support a family of five while I undertook a three-year course of study. We committed the decision and all the need to the Lord, and as we prayed we began to feel certain that if he wanted us to pursue this vocation he would make it possible.

I met with the bishop early in 1981 to express my interest in the priesthood and within six months, after an exhausting bank of interviews, screening exams, and a visit with the diocesan Commission on Ministry, I was made a postulant for holy orders. Meanwhile I had contacted Nashotah House, an Episcopal seminary about thirty miles west of Milwaukee. We sold our home, moved to an on-campus apartment, and began studies that fall.

The founders of Nashotah House were strongly influenced by the Oxford Movement, a mid-nineteenth century renewal in the Church of England led by John Henry Newman, E.B. Pusey, and John Keble. These men believed that theology must not be read in isolation from the worshiping community but that prayer and study ought to be done in tandem. And so at Nashotah, the chapel of St. Mary the Virgin is the center of seminary life. Following a hundred-year-old tradition, seminarians gather each day for the Eucharist and for Morning and Evening Prayer. The whole school moves in rhythm with this regimen of common prayer.

I came to Nashotah for this regimen. I felt that I knew the Scriptures well, but I knew that I also needed to put down roots in the rich soil of the Anglican tradition to find a solid framework for my faith. Gradually, this has happened. I have given myself to the disciplines of the House and to that great compendium of spiritual direction, the Book of Common Prayer. I have received in return the structure I sought, an Anglican body through which my soul now lives and works and prays.

This has had the added effect of giving a strong sense of connectedness to the extended church, which is a new experience for me. In my former tradition I had learned to stand aloof from the church, to keep it at arm's length lest I be implicated in or defiled by her impurities.

In the end I joined the Anglican church not because it was a better church or because the Anglican people are better people. For me it was a turning away from the lure of schism, a turning toward the center, an act of solidarity with all the people of God in all their dazzling and sometimes scandalous variety. There came a time not long ago when I decided that I was either going to have to give up on all the church, every part of it, or I was going to have to turn and embrace all of her, this glorious and notorious lady, the "leprous bride of Christ." I was going to have to give up my heretical hope of having Christ without the church, the Head without the members, the Bridegroom without the bride. Cyprian had said it, changing the image slightly: "He who would have God for his father must have the Church for his mother."

* * *

When I was a young boy back in South Dakota, there was a large billboard which you could see driving eastbound on old highway 50 toward our town. The white letters on the sky-blue sign said simply: "For Peace of Mind Investigate the Catholic Faith." The power of the message—I must have seen it a thousand times—was that it was not a threat, not a demand, not even a promise. It was a quiet invitation and I responded to it.

The church is like that. She sits like a great stone cathedral heavy on the earth—the great, unarguing church. She does not insist on her own importance, and like her Lord, she does not answer back. Simply by being what she is, she summons all who will to step through her always open doors. What is this strange attraction, this mysterious magnetism? It is only that she exalts her Lord, raising up before us all the one who said, "And I, when I am lifted up from the earth will draw all men to myself" (John 12:32).

8.

James Johnson

It happened at Sunday dinner. It was November 1982. Just the three of us there . . . my wife, Rosemary, our son, Jay, who was a junior at Wheaton College . . . myself.

The conversation focused on the matter of catching up on Jay's activities at the college; and then it shifted, as it often did lately, to his experiences at St. Barnabas Episcopal Church. He had been attending there for more than a year, and though we didn't understand why he opted to leave our evangelical church for that, he seemed particularly challenged and excited about his experiences there.

Rosemary and I had been members in our own evangelical church in Wheaton for more than twenty years. All of our Christian lives, some thirty years, were of a similar tradition.

However, in my years of international travel, both as director of an international literature development agency and as an author who did on-site research for all of my novels, I had come to a greater tolerance of the "other sheep." But even with that, I was not sure where Episcopalians stood on the major doctrines.

In his sophomore year at Wheaton, Jay had visited St. Barnabas and found in it something of real value for his own life. We expected his time there to be a "phase," any number of which college students go through in finding their own identity. Or maybe this was a part of an academic exercise in keeping with his church history courses. But as time went on, it became more and more obvious to us that it was more than "academic." He had found something deeper than he had ever experienced in the evangelical conservative community.

The more he talked about it the more Rosemary and I felt a bit concerned. Our Christian experience was tied to the Baptist or Bible church tradition. Our Bible and theology training had been at Moody Bible Institute. Jay, likewise, had come to know Christ in the evangelical church. So we had come to conclude that "it was the only way" for anyone to become a Christian. Or, perhaps more accurately, we felt that the evangelical church was the only ecclesiastical institution that could maintain a Christian's faith and loyalty to God. To depart from it and move toward any other tradition, whether Anglican, Catholic, or whatever we felt was "outside," constituted a "departure" from the true faith.

Yet, on this Sunday Jay was even more articulate about his experience at St. Barnabas. So, because I was growing more curious and perhaps constrained to "correct" his journey in that direction, I simply asked him to give me an example of a positive difference between the Episcopal tradition and our own church.

He seemed ready for the question, having taken a course in worship at Wheaton College that analyzed orthodox worship and liturgies. So he asked, "What is the difference between God-centered and man-centered worship?" I had not really thought about it. My first reaction was that he was referring to the "pseudo-Messiahs" like Sun Myung Moon or Jim Jones, or any man who set himself up as God or a God-figure. I asked him if he meant that.

"No," he said with a half smile, as if he knew that would be my reaction. "Man-centered means that too many Christians put all of their focus in worship on a man, a preacher as it were, and tend then to put less on God." I could understand the rightness of that, but sensing I did not grasp the totality of his statement, he added, "It's like this . . . you are a preacher and you invite another guest speaker to share your pulpit. During the singing and the solo and so forth, the guest speaker leans over to you and says, 'Keep the preliminaries short, I have a lot to say.' That," he concluded, "is man-centered. God was shoved aside there as preliminary for the main event which was the man-preacher."

I pondered it and then said, "Well, was that guest preacher really saying that his preaching was not God-centered?"

"Probably not . . . the point is that his view of worship was not God-oriented. And in the end, the congregation likewise was focusing on him more than on God."

"So wouldn't they see God as much in the preaching of the Word?"

"Insofar as God reveals himself in that, yes. But did the people miss the real focus of worship in opting out for the preaching only? Was the man-centered focus denying the people a proper participation in that worship that would bring God more clearly into view?"

I sensed Rosemary watching me, waiting for the answer to properly negate the proposition and hopefully reinforce the preaching of the Word as the cardinal point of a believer's worship. And that everything prior to the preaching—a couple of hymns, a prayer, the offering, announcements, and so on—were mainly preparation for that.

But I realized right then that I was not on firm ground. Jay had said something I had not considered before. I seldom, if ever, admitted there was anything within the evangelical tradition that was missing or not in line. I had pastored for five years and had carried worship services that I felt were "proper" and, in keeping with that, laid down in heaven. But age and experience has a way of proving that a "closed mouth gathers no foot" at times. I chose now to keep my foot out of my mouth.

I responded simply by saying, "You may have a point. I'll have to think about it."

So after dinner, in my study, I did. I reviewed where I had been or come through in the years past. I had come to know Christ for my life at Moody Church, February 18, 1951. I met Rosemary there a few months later. She had experienced conversion in a Baptist church in St. Clair, Michigan, when she was sixteen. She attended Moody Bible Institute and graduated in 1949. We were married in June 1952. In that time at Moody

Church in Chicago, we had the privilege of sitting under some great preachers. The result of it was our commitment to missionary service in Lagos, Nigeria, West Africa, with the Sudan Interior Mission in 1955.

We served three years there, during which I edited a popular monthly Christian magazine with a circulation of 150,000. In those years, I came to know spiritual development and the priority of biblical study as the key to maturity. The preaching of the Word, whether for Evangelism or discipleship in keeping with the missionary role, became central to the fulfillment of our purpose as Christians. And that has not totally changed.

After the three years, we returned home where I assumed the pastorate of LaSalle Street Church in Chicago. There, I developed my order of service around the priority of the preaching as I had been taught. The rich experiences that came out of our two years there will never be forgotten; they too became times of growth for us and a new realization of Body life that we needed.

After two years of preaching, I felt constrained to return to the University of Michigan to finish my journalism degree. We moved there in September 1961 . . . Jay was born on the 27th. A few months later, we started a new church in the community in response to a number of people who wanted more Bible study approaches to their church life.

In all of these pastoral experiences I maintained a preacher-centered church service. I felt people came to hear the Word, to be blessed from it, to find Christ, then to grow in faith. I have no reason to doubt that God used those years to accomplish his purposes through Rosemary and I.

But now in 1982 and going into 1983, I began to pick around what Jay had said. Was it possible that I, in my years of service as a pastor or even as a parishioner, had been guilty of hiding God behind a veil of "preliminaries"? I was not conscious of that. But, then, could that account for why so many people in Wheaton, and elsewhere, moved from one church to another in search of a "man or a preacher," mistaking that for the search for God?

Yet, it seemed a bit late in my life for me to be pondering such possibilities. By now, I'd had thirty years of service in and for the church. I had taught for fifteen years at Wheaton College Graduate School, had been director of an evangelical international publishing agency for twenty, and had authored twelve books. Why should I now become somewhat curious and a bit disturbed about "God-centered and man-centered" worship? But, then, did the pursuit of God ever really end as long as I had life or breath? On the other hand, was not all of this pure semantics anyway?

Still, could it be possible that I was missing something? Did Jay actually find a dimension in his liturgical experience that Rosemary and I had missed in our years?

In keeping with my journalism discipline, I decided to find out for myself and attend St. Barnabas to better understand what Jay was talking about. Rosemary, sensing she too needed to know more to better exchange experiences with Jay or at least understand his, decided to do likewise.

So on Christmas Eve, a few weeks later, we attended a service. I was struck with the smallness of the sanctuary first. Being used to large auditoriums in a number of churches, I took a few moments to adjust to the atmosphere. The sanctuary was simple in design. Rather austere even. No plush decor. Floors were of plain cement, the pews were wooden and had no cushions. Obviously bodily comfort was not the priority. The sanctuary was built in a semi-circle facing into the nave so that everyone could focus directly on the altar, which was made of simple gray stone. All of the "architectural aesthetics" were subdued—from the dark, rough-hewn cedar beams to the plain, orange-red brick walls.

The service opened with the processional of the choir singing carols as they entered, followed by the acolytes (Jay among them), then the chancel bearers, and finally the priest. The procession was one of solemn dignity and reverence, underscoring the holiness of the sanctuary. And wasn't that what this was supposed to be like anyway? Could one dare to enter the sanctified and holy place set apart for God in any other way? Yet, I had not created such an atmosphere in my years of pastoring, and now I wondered why.

But when the liturgy began, Rosemary and I lost our way immediately as we tried to follow the proper readings in the Book of Common Prayer, or find the hymn listed in one of the two hymnals. All of the time I searched, I was conscious of people kneeling, crossing themselves, the priest chanting the scriptures or the prayers. The Scripture lessons were taken from the Old and New Testament (Epistles) and the Gospels. I had to smile at this, realizing that the average church member in my own evangelical conservative culture, including myself, would find such lengthy readings a bit long and ponderous.

Then came the sermon, and I settled back for this "main event" with some anticipation. The priest stood off to one side on a small platform behind a plain wooden lectern. He was not the "center" of the worship as this arrangement declared; that center was the altar itself.

The sermon was short and simple, a rather subdued homily on the birth of Christ that did not go much beyond fifteen minutes. It was nothing at all like those in my own evangelical tradition in terms of length or audio-visual impact. Yet, there was profundity in the simplicity of the message, truths that even I had not caught in all my years of studying and preaching from those familiar Christmas passages out of Luke and Matthew. *Then it began to dawn on me that the message was only a small part of the whole worship service.* It fit into a synchrony of words with symbols and rituals, all designed to unveil God in his nature, being, and love. I could not follow all of the meaning of those orchestrated parts, nor could I make all the connections they conveyed. But I was intrigued.

Following the sermon, there was the "peace," when the priest said, "The peace of the Lord be with you," and the congregation responded, "And also with you." Then everyone turned to each other and shook hands or embraced, saying, "The peace of the Lord to you." I looked at my wife, not sure what I should do; we had never hugged each other in a church service before! Finally, seeing that everyone else did, and wanting not to stand out as rigid and non-communicative, we did too. And others shook our hands as well. I nodded, mumbled "peace" to them, and hoped I came across as not feeling embarrassed. In this gesture, however, I felt a sense of warmth and friendship, something that perhaps the disciples felt when they were with Christ in the Upper Room. The gestures were genuine and uncomplicated, not forced. Nobody asked me *first* if I was Episcopalian or even a believer. If I had not been a Christian, if I had been a stranger with no understanding of the experience of God in my life, I think I would still have felt welcome and close to God at that moment.

From that part, we moved into the "liturgy of the Eucharist," as my bulletin stated. From then on it was a mixture of sounds and movements at the altar—more chanting of the Scriptures, bells ringing, and incense floating in a mystical blue cover over it all. I felt a bit confused, then somewhat resistant. I didn't know why at first. I had been raised a Lutheran and knew something about liturgy. But this was a much higher form and more difficult to follow. Rosemary had no background in it at all, so I could sense what she must be feeling. I forced myself to pry loose from being threatened by the rituals and from any prejudices I had about such worship form. Instead, I tried to concentrate on the meaning of the rituals and symbols.

As the worship moved on through the sacrament of the Communion, and even as I partook of the bread and wine, I felt a closeness with others, people I had never met before. Some were dressed formally, others in blue jeans. Dress didn't matter here. What mattered was the communion with God.

I was fascinated by it, but still unsure. A bit wary perhaps. Rosemary and I were making a quantum leap from our traditional evangelical, more free-wheeling type of service to the formal, and our minds could not totally shift with it as we would like. I kept asking myself: Is this what Christ had in mind when he said, "They that worship him must worship him in spirit and in truth" (John 4:23)? Or again: Was not all this panoply of images and symbols but a form of medievalism that kept Christ hidden rather than revealed? Were not these symbols and rituals becoming the objects of worship rather than God whom they were supposed to represent? And, more seriously, were the people here placing their faith in the rituals, counting on the symbols and exercises of worship to be the guarantee of their redemption in Christ?

I had to admit I was impressed, even though not convinced. The question that kept bobbing up was: Did this "God-centered" worship give me reason to believe that it was the missing link in the worship life of the evangelical, myself included?

Rosemary and I did not say much on the way home. We were both mulling over the whole situation, wondering at what we had observed, what we had received, what it all meant.

I was not sure I wanted to pursue any more meanings in the service, or even go through it again. A mind and life conditioned by familiar form, especially in religion, is far less prone to cultivate departures from it in order to prove a point. Man is tied to the comforts of traditional, familar patterns and cermonies governing everything from the way he sleeps, eats, works, even to the particular route he takes when driving home from the office . . . and certainly to the familiar in religious form. To deliberately seek to examine other ways is portent to a departure from the norm. And that creates considerable stress. With that, as well, comes a shift in friendships along with the loss of security in what is predictable and acceptable. And in any change of religious habit, for me anyway, there comes the nagging feeling that part of "legitimate" Christianity is sliding away as well.

But Rosemary and I both felt it was still premature to make any final judgments at that point, based on our feelings alone. We had just taken a dive into a pool of ice water. We had come up in shock, blowing and snorting some, but we needed a few more plunges to allow ourselves a more calm approach to the liturgical form. We both concluded we were not being fair in simply writing it off as something alien to our Christian faith or church life. We decided to continue to test the ground to see if God himself was, after all, trying to reveal something to us, even as he had to Jay.

We attended three more times, and each time we experienced the same sense of ambivalence; we felt some of the same awe during the liturgy but doubt kept us distant. I began dissecting the parts I felt were "safe" for my own evangelical conservative tradition—choir, announcements, sermon—and pushing aside those that seemed foreign, confusing, and counter to my own evangelical disciplines.

But I realized that in my dissection of the parts, I was in fact denying the wholeness of what the worship was seeking to convey. In so doing, it did not dawn on me that I might well be fracturing the experience God intended for me.

We took to visiting our own church two of the four Sundays of the month, seeking to maintain our ties and hold to what we believed was "the only way." We felt comfortable there, and at home. But in early February 1983, as I sat in my own evangelical church and stared ahead at the platform where all the action took place, I began to make comparisons. Everything going on in front of me seemed right. It was familiar. The platform was crowded with pastors waiting their turn; the choir was crowded up behind them, staring out at the congregation even as I stared back at them. I felt the comfortable blue velvet cushions under me, the gleaming white chandeliers above me, the royal blue carpeting down the aisle. It was a decor I had known most of my Christian life in the churches I had visited as a member or speaker, even as a pastor, though LaSalle Street Church was more like St. Barnabas in its furnishings. Still, I had no reason to question any of those surface things.

But I began to feel some uneasiness. It wasn't in the order of service, the purposes of this church I had known for twenty years in my evangelical tradition. I myself had pastored in similar sanctuaries, and carried out the same order of service. The people here were genuine too. They knew God. They were faithful to him and committed. Rosemary and I had been recipients of their true friendship and love in so many meaningful ways through the years there.

So why was I trying to pick an irritating piece of lint off my brain on this day?

The music stopped, the offering was taken, the announcements delivered. And it was time for the preacher. The congregation seemed to sink a little deeper into the cushions in anticipation. This was the moment, after all, that they had come for—the preaching, the "main event." Forty-eight minutes later he finished the sermon. Now it was time to shake hands on the way out, car keys held in one hand. Dinner was on!

On the way home, I did not feel much of anything. Was I supposed to? No one had failed me. The preacher had done his work and fairly well. So had everyone else. They had "put on a service" and by all standards I knew, it had been properly done and the Word delivered.

So why the continuing feeling of uneasiness? I was beginning to compare it with the worship at St. Barnabas. Maybe what I had in my own church was too predictable, too familiar? Maybe after all the years of that familiarity one becomes narcotized by a form that does not penetrate deep enough to give the soul cause to wonder or be in awe? Was that it? And I realized then that in that whole service God did not pass before my eyes. I heard the words, the music, but for most of the time I stared at the backs of people's heads, counting pimples on necks, tracing contours of ears and staring at gold dew-drop earrings. And all the time I was trying to concentrate on the words while glancing furtively at my watch.

Was I then going into a flat line in my soul or in my Christian experience? It was not totally a disinterest in the words or whatever passed for worship time but mainly a consciousness of an absence of something. Had St Barnabas Episcopal opened a door that I could not now fully close? Had that brief experience there sprung a hole in the bow of my "good ship *grace*," and was I now sliding under?

No. Instead, the words "man-centered" and "God-centered" popped to the surface of my mind again. Was it all that simple? Could it really be the root of my uneasiness, even dissatisfaction with a worship form I had known all my life as a Christian and as a pastor? Maybe I was supposed to make that service in my own church a "God-centered" experience in my own mind even though the service was mostly "man-centered." Maybe I was supposed to do that work on my own rather than make it the responsibility of those who led the service? I wondered how many other Christians were going home as I did that day, feeling a little bit unfulfilled. It was like a kind of ennui had pervaded, a sense of having missed a point of spiritual energy that should have been there but was not. Who does one blame for that? Nobody.

I remained a bit troubled for the next two weeks. Rosemary was experiencing similar contrary signals too—being at the church we had known for twenty years, the tradition we had known for thirty, but not really coming away with that "thing" neither of us could identify.

Then, on Jay's advice we decided to attend the Ash Wednesday service at St. Barnabas a few weeks later. This is the beginning of Lent in the Anglican tradition. I never had been to an Ash Wednesday service in my life. Ashes on people's foreheads were a sign of another ecclesiastical tradition. I remembered some of my Catholic friends with whom I had grown up coming to school sporting that smear of black like it was some kind of badge of honor God had bestowed for faithful attendance. Yet, I did not feel any prejudice toward them because of it; only that same question: "Was all that necessary?"

So on that Wednesday night in St. Barnabas, I was somewhat defensive about it all as we sat in the sanctuary. It was almost in total darkness, except for one or two candles around the altar—symbolic of the beginning of Christ's forty days of suffering in the flesh, from the Upper Room, to Gethsemane, then the cross. The darkness felt eerie, but the sense of being caught up in the despair that Christ must have felt in his darkest hour came home with palpable reality. There was a stillness in the place, a holy hush, a feeling of acute awareness of what Christ faced in his final hours on earth.

All of this kind of snuck up on me, and before I could analyze the feelings, I was in it. I was not looking at a choir now, though they sang from the right somewhere in very soft, subdued notes. I was not aware of anyone around me. I felt that something was happening here. It was not a single action or movement. The Scriptures were read but I did not see the reader nor even bother to look for whoever it was . . . I was praying aloud with others from the Book of Common Prayer but I heard only my own voice . . . I sang from the hymnal, but I heard only my own discordant notes. The movements of those who served at the altar were slow, quiet, reverent—keeping the sacred hour of silence as a vigil.

I sensed, when the service was finished, that I had, for the first time in my Christian life, entered fully into Lent and its meaning; into the sorrows of Christ, sorrows he took for me. I felt I had joined with him in those brief movements, and he had communicated something vital of himself to me, something of the cost of redemption. After all the years I had preached on Holy Week and given exegetical studies on the meaning of those last days of Christ, I had not fully grasped it until now.

Nobody was preaching at me. Nobody was testifying to the truth of it; nobody was manipulating that truth through dramatic atmosphere. It had all come through the sense of his presence via the palpable symbol of darkness.

When the priest gave his brief message, every word seemed pregnant with the meaning of the darkness Christ had faced. All that had gone before enlarged that message so that, brief as it was, the emphasis was made by the Spirit himself. When the communion was served, I felt a new reality in the symbols of the bread and wine, the "broken bread and poured out wine," the sacrifice given by Christ for me. I had known all of this as truth in my twenty five years of Christian living; it had been the basis of my conversion experience. But tonight, on this Ash Wednesday 1983, I felt that a dimension of that experience had come to life.

Why? Much later, I had to agree, Christ had become the center of that simple service. Every part, every element, every symbol, every ritual pulled aside the veil and allowed him to be revealed as he wanted to be.

So I took the black smear on my forehead, the sign of my identification with his hour of darkness. And I did not rub it off in a hurry either. It became a symbol, one more; but much deeper, it became a sign of my understanding of the darkest hour he spent for me.

Rosemary felt much the same experience. And because we shared similar feelings, there developed in us a desire to journey further, to understand even more of this mystery, this form of worship that drew out total beings into the reality of confrontation with him.

All of which motivated me to read and research, the disciplines I knew as an author. I picked up Dr. Robert Webber's book *Common Roots—A Call to Evangelical Maturity* (Zondervan, 1978), in which he looks at "historic Christianity" in terms of the worship experience. I chose Webber's book because I had known him as a friend and a fellow professor at Wheaton College. His experience was similar to ours in that he too had found an empty spot in the evangelical church's area of worship. And he had taken the same journey.

I gained a lot of insight and confirmation about my experience in his book. One thing, among many other explanations he presented about worship, confirmed what had been bothering me when comparing the two worship forms—those I knew in my own evangelical church and those in St. Barnabas. He said, " . . . In a full service of worship, the entire spectrum of Christian faith is included. Worship is a rehearsal of who God is and what he has done, and gives expression to the relationship which exists between God and his people. The focus of content in a sermon alone, or the emphasis found among the renewal churches where worship centers around a single aspect of God or a theme, misses the point of worship and fails to worship God in his entirety . . . in summary the historic Christian approach to worship which emphasized the adoration of the Father through the Son has been replaced in some churches by a program with a stage and an audience. . . . "

These words, I felt, put the finger on it for me. I knew that some people like the stage and the program. But for others, there is a deeper need, and that had been met for me in that Ash Wednesday service at St. Barnabas.

I moved on to Webber's book *Worship Old and New* (Zondervan, 1981) and noticed his reference to the "imbalance of worship" that "lies in its overidentification with rationalism, emotionalism, or entertainment . . . the emphasis on the mind—on a thoughtful, reflective, cognitive approach to worshiping God. This approach usually emphasizes the understanding of the Word. Scripture reading is sometimes accompanied by explanation. Sermons are always exegetical, emphasizing the meaning of the text, sometimes without application to the hearer. Other congregations display a tendency to overemphasize the emotional element. This approach to worship focuses on the feelings—the immediate experience of God that results in feeling good about being in church."

"True worship," he adds, "does stimulate the mind, move the emotions and produces a sense of fun . . . but worship ought not to be reduced to a lecture hall, a psychiatric couch, or a stage."

But then he underscored why the symbols and rituals work as they do to enlarge Christ in worship maintaining the "Christocentric focus" of the church in worship. This "actualization of the church in worship," as he puts it, brings in all "the physical signs of Christ's presence and these signs signify the spiritual reality they represent." The darkness at Ash Wednesday, the candles on Christmas Eve, and so on were means God used to help me grasp spiritual reality in worship.

Having studied both of Dr. Webber's books (and I refer only to a few paragraphs that confirmed what I was experiencing at St. Barnabas), I had come to a better and even a new understanding of why I had missed far too much in conducting worship in the evangelical church. I knew now, more than before, that in order to "see God" there needed to be an entirely new approach in the use of palpable, identifiable symbols in the world through which he can be "seen." I knew likewise that the

Scriptures state that "no one has ever seen God; the only Son, who is in the bosom of the Father, he has made him known" (John 1:18). No one has seen him *corporally;* but it does not mean he can't be seen in the human and symbolic relational levels he has chosen.

To experience the "seeing" of him in this way, one has to move into the realm of the symbolic and *trust* it. For instance, incense used in the Anglican form of worship is a symbol of God's holiness or perfection. . . . Its sweet smell and softness of cloud convey a form of himself that could not be seen as well without it.

But if no attempt is made to build relational experiences that reveal God, as Dr. Webber states, "current evangelical worship tends to be passive—the believer sits in the pew waiting for something to be done for him and to him. In evangelical worship we sing, put money in the plate, and sometimes say Amen. If the relationship of these responses, minimal as they are to the whole activity of worship, was understood, it would make worship more meaningful."

The point is that there is not much to be understood in the present evangelical worship as I conducted so often and which is conducted by so many of my ministerial brethren. There are few attempts to bring a relational level to any of it; and there are no familiar identifiable signs, symbols, or rituals that finite man can understand in terms of a revelation of some part of God himself.

But further, as I found in my own journey, another fundamental reason for this failure or refusal perhaps (although like myself many evangelical pastors long for a meaningful worship time for their people) is that too many Christians operate on the principle that God is summed up in a mathematical formula $2 + 2 = 4$. This is the "thus saith the Lord" approach, which, while it has its point in terms of the authority of Scripture, cannot hold up in any attempt to reveal God in worship. In this, God is locked into a one-dimensional level of exposure of himself, if indeed he can be revealed at all in a mathematically dogmatic sense. God did not create the world on a slide rule, in other words, nor did he compute the elements of nature or the mixtures that would go into the creation of man purely on a statistical level.

I was struck again that God is an artist, not a mathematician, at least in terms of his own creative genius. All that was created comes from his own artistic sensitivity. One only has to look around the material world—let alone man himself—to realize this. This is the value of symbols, rituals, incense, bells—those relational objects that we all recognize in his attempt to reveal himself.

The other problem that follows this then is that as evangelicals—and I speak and judge myself now more so than anyone else in my community—we suspect form in worship as not being necessary or perhaps not "spiritual." "Form" belongs to medieval times, to state churches, Roman churches, or those religious people in "black hats." We too often conclude that saying the Lord's Prayer and singing the Doxology is the maximum form of worship we dare allow. It's a start toward true worship, of course, but it still falls way short in terms of amplifying the revelation of God. Again, the failure to expand on this may be due to the mind set that says these are "preliminaries" and must not take away from the preaching. Or, in some cases, it smacks of a formality that does not fit the relaxed atmosphere of a church on friendly terms with God.

But form, as I concluded in my experience at St. Barnabas, was too close to religious traditions I had abandoned when I became a true Christian. To counter that, I reverted back to the simplistic, prosaic 2 + 2 = 4 approach even when I realized, as do many of my brethren and sisters, that God cannot reveal himself through that limited formula.

There is a beauty in worship, which is the front porch for understanding the mystical, because it appeals to the aesthetic senses. And if so, then there must be necessary, identifiable elements through which to convey that. It means moving into the realm of the aesthetics, relying on the symbolic that communicates relational aspects of God's attributes. Otherwise, then, there is only the repetition of the cognitive, that which Webber calls worship only in the "mind." Even as the painter and the writers seek to bring all the colors and all the metaphors and similies to bear on ellucidating the truth of life, so, then, there must be the same employment if we are to reveal God or allow him to be revealed.

The trap I had fallen into in my years as a pastor in the evangelical community, and even as a parishioner too, was to make conversion an automatic, perpetuating, "all seeing" experience; so there was no need then to pursue God in worship. I mistakenly concluded that "seeing" came totally from within, along the scriptural line that "they who worship him must worship him in spirit and in truth" (John 4:23). While I did that, I was depending totally on an internal spiritual view, and whether I could say I had "seen" God in worship that day or not was immaterial. I am a Christian, therefore I must see. But did I? I needed these tangible and concrete elements to bring my mind, heart, my emotions to bear on the associations related to and about God. I thus became poorer as time went by, because I did not.

It comes down to what Webber concludes, "For evangelicals, the restoration of public worship may involve the rethinking of the order of worship toward a more inclusive rehearsal of the entire faith, an increased use of the Lord's supper as the focal point of worship, and a return to a creative use of the church year. Perhaps in this way we will be able to overcome the man-centeredness and the lack of content which has helped create the yearning for a more fulfilling experience of worship."

Two years later, since that first Christmas Eve experience at St. Barnabas, and eighteen months after that memorable Ash Wednesday service, the gate has swung wider. There is now forming, and in some cases already formed, the answer to the missing link in my own worship experience as an evangelical.

Friends and fellow pastors have asked if Rosemary and I have "departed from the evangelical faith" in taking this journey. This thinking exacerbates the problems and tensions that exist in the ecclesiastical adherences so many feel are a priority even in knowing God. No, we have not "departed," whatever that means. We have found a ground that is new to us yet, but it is ground upon which we have "seen the glory." Our concern is to transplant some of that back into the evangelical church life. The evangelical community has, and always will have, much to commend it, that which we hold to this day: evangelistic zeal, a cleavage to biblical authority, and a level of commitment that has shaped entire cultures and populations for Christ. The Episcopal church has much of the same, but its emphasis on meaningful and revelational worship is one distinct aspect that evangelicals would do well to emulate.

If the intelligent and spiritually sensitive minds in both communities could recognize what each has to give the other, and if there was a literal breaking down of the man-made artificial walls that separate on sectarian lines, there could be a spiritual shaking that would undoubtedly cause the world to ponder.

So I would embrace all brethren and sisters who know the living Christ—whatever flag they choose to travel under in the name of God—and simply urge all to get on this kind of journey on their own.

I thank God that our son, Jay, had the courage to pursue his. And then, likewise, the courage to share with us what he had found. I would be derelict not to emulate his concerns for Rosemary and me—by pursuing a deeper experience with God in this way and help others to do the same.

As Dr. Webber so aptly put it, "We must learn, then, not to *have* a spirituality, something we turn on at a particular place or time, but to *be* spiritual, as a habit of life, a continuous state of being. It is to this end that we seek after God in the stillness and the hubbub of life, but always and everywhere in and through the church, where Christ is made present for us, and through us to the world." Amen!

9.

John Skillen

Recently my wife and I returned to the Church of the Advent, the venerable Anglo-Catholic church in Boston, for the High Mass on the Second Sunday in Advent. Our last visit was many years ago, during our last year as students at Gordon College. Now with graduate school behind us, we have made a journey of return for me to join the faculty of my alma mater. Our trip to the Advent was prompted by the chance to hear Martin Shaw, a Scottish Anglican priest and gifted baritone, sing Vaughan Williams' arrangement of "Five Mystical Songs" by the seventeenth-century Anglican priest and poet, George Herbert. A representative of an earlier "evangelical Anglicanism," Herbert is an iconic figure for me. He was a central figure in a moment of church history that seemed to combine comfortably a Reformed theology based on the touchstone *solas* of the Reformation—Scriptures, faith, grace—with a sacramental imagination and a liturgical spirituality.

Back in the cavernous Gothic-revival vault of the Church of the Advent, I found myself wondering how the place felt to my four-year-old daughter, Jessamine Mary. Was the dark brick sanctuary gloomy or gloriously solemn? I asked her if she liked the smell of the incense and pointed out to her the seven red lamps hanging across the chancel, the ornate stone reredos carved with prophets and apostles, the gaunt and gory Christ on the cross high above the chancel steps, the four-foot statue of Christ the King behind the bank of votive candles, the lofty pulpit spotlighted dramatically during the homily, the purple and gold brocade vestments of the priests, the carved angels behind the choir. I felt the irony of my attempts to nurture an iconographic spirituality in my children, having been nurtured myself in an evangelical home iconoclastically indisposed to the use of visual aids and sensible signs in worship.

I found myself recalling my first visits to the Advent as a college freshman back in 1971 and 1972. Indeed, like Proust's recovery of his childhood in the taste of a cookie dipped in tea, the communion water made present again not only the body of Christ but my own college life. During those five years I had become an Anglican without shedding the fundamentals of my evangelical faith.

But my Proust-image exaggerates. I remember little of my first experiences in the Episcopal church. Of my present parish, Christ Church of Hamilton, attended once or twice in my freshman year, I have only a hazy memory of the white stucco walls and the pulpit tucked oddly to the side as if the sermon were inconsequential. With my roommate Harold Fickett, stringy-haired and in Marxist-Leninist rebellion against the Baptist faith of his fathers, I tagged along to the Advent several times with our Anglophiliac friend, Michael Barwell. My irregularly kept journal doesn't help my memory much, but one passage records some early impressions:

> Susie and I went into the Advent with Michael this morning for the Easter service. We had tea and a muffin before the service, and Susie met some of the weird Anglicans. Such cigarette smoking and impersonal personableness; the Boston nouveau chic; the hypocritical Anglophiles. Susie said, "They all talk the same, and they knock the ashes from their cigarettes in the same way, with a delicate twirl against the side of the ash tray." I see clearly that I cannot enjoy the Advent and participate in the service. I am not a Church of the Advent person. The incense began to make me wheeze and feel lightheaded, and I had to take one of Susie's asthma pills. The pill, and the communion wine, made me feel even more lightheaded, and

by the end of the service I was feeling quite odd and very concerned about my grip on reality. Our ride back with Bob and Sandy Friedrich was silent.

I wish I could find the cynical narrative essay I wrote for Professor Howard's freshman writing class. A Joycean interior monologue of my thoughts while taking communion at the Advent, the story cast doubt on the efficacy of the sacrament for the ritualizers and perverts at the rail. I argued, if I recall, that special acts lose meaning through frequent repetition.

I was clearly no instant convert. Troubled by much at the Advent, I was a reluctant Canterbury pilgrim. So why were my occasional Boston excursions less often to Park Street Church, a well-known evangelical church, and more often to the Church of the Advent? "I went for the sherry hour," says Fickett. And Michael is frank to admit the attraction of the pageantry of the liturgy. But why did Susie and I attend Magnolia Congregational less often and Christ Church of Hamilton more often until, by our senior year, I was an acolyte and we were Episcopalians? Why the growing number of evangelical college students who are attracted to Episcopalian churches? Certainly for many reasons, the aesthetic's and the Anglophiliac's among them. But I think more comprehensive answers can be found. It is not the sherry that attracts students, but the clear light shed on life by the mass, the recovery of authority, catholicity, and ceremony in the liturgy and the sacraments. Indeed, Michael's oft-announced claim, as the only confirmed Anglican convert among us, to be a member of "the one true holy catholic and apostolic church" may provide the best rubric for interpreting the phenomenon.

But my first intention here is to tell my own story and trust it to be representative. I wish to remain faithful to the largely inchoate experience—inarticulate, immature, naïve, and *not* theologically fine-tuned—of the college student. Hence, I suspect it true for most, as it was for me, that specifically denominational positions on issues of church and doctrine are often irrelevant to the collegiate Canterbury pilgrimage. That is, I'm not at all sure that the American Episcopal church is the determining factor, as the conversion of a growing number of evangelical students not only to the Anglican but also to the Roman and Orthodox churches perhaps suggests. Rather, the Episcopal church is the less problematic option for students who remain committed to the fundamentals of evangelical faith, yet find in liturgical and sacramental spirituality a nourishment that they are not receiving in the circles of cultural Evangelicalism.

For me, that freshman essay provides a clue to my own Canterbury Trail. Its stream-of-consciousness narrative illustrates the peculiar self-consciousness that seems always to have beset me, a self-consciousness exacerbated by the available modes of evangelical spirituality, and relieved by the liturgical worship I found in the Anglican church. By self-consciousness I mean an awareness not so much of others looking at me as of *me* looking at me. I have a tendency to lose immersion in an activity and to step back and observe the event and my place in it. But don't we' all have such moments? As a boy, for example, while reading a book I would often become conscious *that* I was reading. I would become interested in understanding the process whereby the sight of black marks on a page could prompt an imaginative presence in the world of *Treasure Island* or *Tom Sawyer*, a presence to which I had lost all sense of deciphering black marks on a page. Of course, the effect of such reflective moments is to stop one from reading. The world of the book is lost and I remember the anxious frustration of trying to lose myself in the book again. But the willful act of trying to read would further promote the conditions precluding reading. A deadly circle.

During my first years at college, for whatever reasons, this tendency toward self-consciousness became the painful and pervasive condition of my everyday state. I've come across a letter I wrote as a freshman to my friend Dave McCurry:

> Now, about awareness, and awareness of awareness. A bit of review: when you are smelling a flower, or tasting tea, or reading, you are not aware of doing these things. At moments of awareness of what you are doing (when you suddenly think, "I am smelling this flower"), then you are not doing it. Well, the number of moments during the day when I have stepped back to observe myself has steadily increased. You see where this leads: at moments of being aware of life, you are not then living . . . What gives a present situation its meaning is the past and future perspective we have on it, plus all the other items in memory and history and experience associated with it. What gives, for instance, a visit with you at

Christmastime its meaning is looking forward to it, remembering it, plus all that has gone into making our friendship. But what has happened to me is that in each present situation, I am aware of all this. I have an "awareness of awareness" that I have been looking forward to such and such, or have hoped for this, or that sometime I will look back on this, etc., etc. Such awareness kills the situation and destroys its meaning. Moments of such self-consciousness have become more and more frequent until last week I saw how very much of life I had destroyed.

A disturbed condition, to be sure, but representative of moments we all have.

Such self-consciousness distances one from involvement in an action. It makes one feel like a foreigner. From a position outside, the activity feels strange and may suddenly appear as the parochial activity of a provincial culture. Moreover, feeling foreign inhibits one's ability to *act*. Unself-conscious involvement in an activity drives it to its conclusion. Immersed in the book, you turn page after page without knowing it. Tasting the cake prompts the next bite. Involved in a familiar dance, you don't think about the steps. One is not "self-conscious" like the beginner, painfully aware of his shuffling feet. The foreigner hesitates at the dinner table to see what the rules of dining decorum are. My point is that any breakdown, any sense of not belonging or of being on the outside, any uncertainty about conventions, inhibits action.

Instances of my own "existential paralysis," prompted by self-consciousness, are painful for me to rehearse. My ears still redden when I recall the crisis of the evening I first held Susie's hand. Aware that, with this simple act of reaching across the table in Gordon's snack shop and taking her hand, I was setting into play an action that, with one thing leading to another, could determine the rest of my life. I was immobilized. After a half hour of mustering up my courage, I made my move. But then it was no longer an act of affection; rather, it was an existential act of the will.

I shall bear the embarrassment of quoting a passage from an old journal, almost psychotic in its self-absorption:

On the way back to school after seeing Polanski's *Macbeth* with Dr. Howard, Steve Meeter, Susie, and Phil Tierney, we were all rather silent. I had some things to say about the movie, and I saw the occasion as one which, if I was silent and didn't act, could be another event leading to my spiritual and mental shrivelling up. Or, if I spoke and attempted intellectual conversation, it could be an event holding off my death and possibly bringing life. I sat there, planning the conversation in my mind, and pondering the act of beginning to speak. An Aaron Copeland work was on the radio, quite awful and too loud. I wanted to tell Phil to turn it down ("Phil, could you turn down the radio . . . "). Then Howard made some comment about the movie, which provided an opening for me to talk about it, and also to ask Phil to turn down the radio. So I sat there, aware of the existential decision, and (important) I knew that I would finally make the decision and speak. (I am learning to make those existential decisions and acts.) I sat there, and made a couple of very shallow preparations for acting. But I let too much time pass for my speaking-start to be related to Howard's comment, and thus to Phil's turning down the radio. So I would have to make a new conversational beginning. This required more preparation and more conversation constructing, which I performed. But still, I had to make four breath-suckings and mouth preparations and body-tensings before I was able to perform the act and throw the words "the film" up out of my throat for my ears to hear. As usual, I had said them over and over and over so that they had a separate existence of their own (not spontaneous utterances of a thought) which required a forceful act of the will to get out.

My sanity may be in doubt, but I spot the same symptoms in my own students, in class, in my office, or at departmental gatherings for our majors.

Nor was my spiritual life immune to the destructive, debilitating "phenomenological gaze." Prayer dissolved into self-reflective analysis of my motives and of the parochial matter and manner of my petitions. Indeed, I was in a crisis of faith, though not in the sense of disbelieving or of blaming God. Aware of having destroyed the fabric of spiritual life, I was anxious and guilt-stricken over my shrivelled and cynical condition. I remember once sobbing while trying to explain to Susie how I had been so beset with self-consciousness during a communion service at the college chapel that I had rendered the act of communion absolutely null and void. Watching myself, observing others, analyzing the service. Dormitory or small group Bible studies were particularly painful. If simple conversation among friends about a movie paralyzed me, think how I felt when expected to share what Christ had done in my life that week. Imagine my anxiety as my turn in the circle of prayer drew relentlessly closer, like the pendulum in Poe's story. Imagine the act of the will required to throw the words "Dear Heavenly Father" out of my throat.

This tendency to self-consciousness accounts in large measure, it seems to me, for my discomfort with an evangelical spirituality, which sets the self center-stage, and hence triggers the very self-consciousness that abstracts one from involvement and inhibits action. Secondly, it explains the appeal of a liturgical worship in which one enters into an act larger than oneself, prior to oneself, and not experientially dependent on oneself and the fervor one brings to it.

Collegiate evangelicalism's focus on the self pinned me wriggling to the wall the first week of freshman year. Having quickly struck up something of a relationship with Susie Johnson, I went with her to a meeting of the Park Street Church college group called "Break Out." Shy and self-conscious, Susie and I were mortified by games such as penny races—waddling to the other end of the hall and back while squeezing a penny between your knees. Such activities, I suppose, are designed to prepare the self for the instant intimacy required by evangelical youth spirituality. First, let's go around the circle, say your name, tell where you're from, and tell how you met the Lord, or, a common variant, share what the Lord's been doing in your life this week. Or out come the guitars. I remember from the "Break Out" group only the song about Charlie stuck forever on the Boston MTA, but the favorites in the dormitory Bible studies and sharing groups were songs such as "We Are One in the Spirit." Everyone joined hands. Mine were cold and clammy, yet, like a ganglia of exposed nerves, sending and receiving waves of uncertain and indecipherable messages.

I remember the "existential crises" prompted by "sharing." There I sat, already aware of life as one hermeneutic rat's nest of conflicting and untrustworthy interpretations of what God's will for my life was, among people whose lingo allowed only certainty. I remember, when prayer time came, the awkward silence while waiting for someone to go first; the angst while waiting to see if the guy beside the first would go next—perhaps establishing a round-the-circle pattern from which there was no escape. Bars atuned, skin alert, sweat glands popping off like howitzers—I was acutely attentive to all vibes *but* those of the Holy Spirit. The prayers too often degenerated into what we now call the "just" prayer: "Lord, we just want to come before you, Lord, and just thank you Lord for just being who you are, and for just being with us, and we just pray that . . . "

It's easy, of course, to caricature, and my intention here is not to satirize or to find hypocrisy in the best of evangelical youth spirituality. The motives behind evangelicalism's focus on the self may be commendable: its zeal to nurture the individual's personal relationship with Christ, to arouse sensitivity to the voice of God, to nurture responsibility for one another through a life together of prayer and intimacy and sharing and emotional honesty. But my concern is that evangelical spirituality has allied itself too closely with the subjectivist notions of modern pop psychology: that the self transparently knows itself; that people *can* instantly and honestly bare their souls to one another; and that to do so is *ipso facto* efficacious.

My point, in sum, is that in my college experience of evangelical spirituality the success of an act of individual or corporate devotion seemed to depend on the fervor we brought to it as individuals. Yet this focus on the self debilitates the self-conscious adolescent stricken with uncertainty about his self.

So there I was, orbiting the world like one of Walker Percy's modern men, seeking a means of reentry. I found it in liturgical worship, although not immediately. My early visits to Episcopal churches left me all the more self-conscious because the setting, the actions, the conventions of worship were foreign. Genuflecting or crossing myself were as impossible to perform as the ritual gestures of evangelical piety. I was as self-conscious walking up the aisle to the altar rail as I was praying in Jim Riley's Bible study back at the dorm. But a slow process of healing began that liberated me from the prison-house of the self. Because I didn't have to focus on myself in the hot-house atmosphere of the sharing group, I could focus on the prayers, the texts, the actions. And they rang true, true to life—oh, how much more so than my own uncertain and inarticulate stops and starts! Nor did the collects and confessions of the Book of Common Prayer come across as the "canned" prayers of someone else. Indeed, they were more *my* prayers.

I have given here a mainly psychological account, based on a self-consciousness exacerbated by evangelical piety, of my attraction to the liturgical and sacramental tradition of the church. But I believe my experience of alienation and abstraction, my uncertainty about how to act, is not idiosyncratic.

One can be confident of his actions only as he can locate them in a community and a tradition that establishes the conventions, for example, of eating, courting, behaving at parties, conversing with elders, or praying. But our age of relativism and individualism is marked precisely by the breakdown of community, the loss of tradition, and the forgetfulness of history. Hence, the "identity crisis" of modern young people is not strictly a psychological phenomenon but a cultural phenomenon. The shapelessness of modern life and the absence of authoritative paradigms is the cause, I think, of the thirst among many young people for the recovery of tradition, of cultural and historical *location*. This is the attraction of the historic traditions of the church, into whose established, time-proven, objective forms of devotion and worship one may enter and find oneself.

To be sure, Evangelicalism itself provides a comfortable tradition for many young people. The happy immersion and loss of self-consciousness of many in typically evangelical sharing times, or services of worship, or KC '83 gatherings, is evidence that those so immersed have found themselves by losing themselves in a tradition with no seams in its fabric. Evangelicalism provides a system of conventions for thought, feeling, action, worship, and devotion apparently adequate to their experience. But I always felt a tension between the self-centering forms of evangelical spirituality and its self-effacing motives.

Thus, while holding to the fundamentals of dogma maintained by evangelicalism, I (and perhaps the typical evangelical convert to Anglicanism) couldn't find a home in the conventions of spirituality afforded by evangelicalism. Playing into the hands of the subjective individualism of modern culture, evangelical piety lacked *authority* just when I needed authoritative words to sort out the chaos of life. For me, a group of nineteen- and twenty-year-olds in a dormitory Bible study sharing what Galatians means to them lacked exegetical authority. I found evangelicalism's apparent trust in the egalitarian methods of the Holy Spirit troubling. I found untrustworthy the shared testimonies of my peers about God's will for their lives. For me, these moments of doubt—the sense that even the appeal to the guidance of the Holy Spirit was no sure defense against individual interpretation of God's Word and will—helped prompt the attraction to a liturgical worship based on objective act and dogma.

In any case, liturgical worship allowed me to forget myself in a corporate action not contingent on my own feelings at the moment for its effect. The efficacy of the liturgy does depend on *faith*, but efficacy resides within the corporate *act*, performed in faith, rather than in the faith as evidenced in the subjective *feelings* of the individuals present. Participation in liturgical worship frees the self from its own subjective self-consciousness and places him in a "work of the people," as liturgy means, larger than his own private acts of piety. Invited to experience the ordering shape of the liturgy, I experienced not constriction but a liberation. And lo and behold, submission to the liturgy prompted the recovery of personal involvement and of pious feelings. That the liturgical work was performing a work of healing dawned on me suddenly, I recall, when I noticed that I wept at the Eucharist, and when tears of joy and zeal came to my eyes as we followed the cross out into the world in "strength and courage to love and serve" the crucified and resurrected Christ.

Moreover, the liturgy itself announces its nature as a work of the people more encompassing than the 200 within the walls of Christ Church of Hamilton or the Church of the Advent. The liturgy expands outward in both space and time. One is performing the same act, rehearsing the same drama of salvation, with Christians in the next town, in far distant countries, and in far distant times. It is an ancient liturgy, originating in the shape of the liturgy of the apostolic church. Indeed, one performs in the liturgy the sacramental act inaugurated by Christ that constitutes the church. What I am trying to describe here is my adolescent experience of *catholicity*, which relocates the stranded self in a larger enterprise. For me, the sense of catholicity renders the worship authoritative and the experience of the self who participates in it trustworthy.

But might not any large group give the same feel of catholicity? What is the difference between the experience of catholicity afforded by a small congregation of an historic church whose liturgy and sacrament has legitimate catholic pretensions, and, say, a local chapter of an international organization such as Inter-Varsity, or a 5,000 member Los Angeles Baptist Church, or an Urbana or KC '83 gathering of thousands? Why, before I gave much thought to catholicity and authority, did I feel more a part of a catholic church among 200 at Christ Church than among 18,000 at Urbana '70? One reason is that true catholicity never has the quality of being staged. Catholicity is not conjured up; it exists. The church does not create its catholicity; it is obedient to it. I was troubled by feelings of unity and catholicity that appeared to be produced by the emotional immediacy of the event.

If my experience is representative, the typical collegiate evangelical convert to Anglicanism is one who is troubled by the absence of authority in the emotional and egalitarian spirituality of evangelicalism. The larger cultural context of his desire for authoritative words, for reentry into tradition and history, is the flattened, plotless, shapeless world of modernity. He seeks diagrams and paradigms that clarify and *name* life, its purpose, its narrative shape. I found such paradigms in the Anglican liturgy, which, with visual clarity and verbal precision rehearse the drama of our creation, fall, and redemption.

Here I can mention a final reason for my attraction to the Episcopal church. I enjoyed liturgical and sacramental worship for its authority and catholicity, but also for its holiness, its solemnity, its ceremony. Liturgy and sacrament provided a means for recovering the ceremony of life. The appeal of liturgical pageantry and ceremony cannot be explained away as an aesthetic pleasure alone. Rather, the liturgy satisfies what I call the craving for signs felt by many in the nominalistic desert of modernity.

Unable to render experience significant through signs, people have no way to mark, to signify, to name the important events or the strongest feelings of life. Indeed, without signposts, one can discern no "plot" in life. Sneakers are proper attire to all events when all events occupy the same bottom rung on the hierarchy of experience. The point should be pressed. Signs enable us not only to solemnify the great issues of life but to *see* those issues. The liturgy for the Solemnization of Matrimony, for instance, not only expresses a significance we may already feel, but proclaims a significance we may not feel. Without signs one can discern no hierarchy in the values of one's strong feelings. If no one labels the difference, for example, between love and lust, if no one, that is, names the signs by which the two are distinguished, then how can the young person discern the difference?

Here again, I worry that the collegiate evangelical culture offers not only a casual set of conventions for devotion and piety, but also a watered-down set of traditional, orthodox, Christian labels. Evangelical spirituality focuses too often on getting in touch with one's feelings, rather than judging the propriety of those feelings. It lacks a clear sense that feelings are inchoate and untrustworthy unless properly labeled.

Liturgical and sacramental worship is attractive, I am suggesting, because it provides an iconographic realm where things and actions *signify,* and signify richly, not through any private symbolism but through traditional, historic, public, and therefore authoritative, symbolism. The liturgy provides a diagram of life and the world in which, again, "everything serves to exemplify." In the liturgy, we enter into signs. The pressure is off; we don't have to invent them. It's a party where the rules are clearly set down. One doesn't feel awkward in kneeling to confess, or in public confession itself, because everyone is doing it. The signs teach us as well. They not only promote, but prompt, the actions and conditions toward which they point us. I may not, for example, feel like confessing my sins. I may, in fact, feel I have no pressing sin to confess. But the act of confession reminds us of what is *true:* "we have sinned against you in thought, word, and deed." I may not feel like blessing God, but singing the Gloria or the Te Deum prompts the act. I may not feel the bonds of charity binding the brotherhood in Christ, or I may not feel like acting on those bonds, but the Passing of the Peace—which establishes the conditions of our corporate act of Eucharist—teaches me what is true of the body of Christ.

Thus, I found in the Anglican liturgy an authoritative naming of the issues of existence, and a clear diagram of the plot of the Christian life. I found through its paradigmatic gestures and statements a means of solemnifying the issues of life. Moreover, the experience of liturgical worship provided a tutor which taught me how to ceremonialize the rest of life. This last point is difficult to explain, but I know that my wife and I can now host a dinner party, that we can successfully enact a Christmas "ritual" for our young daughters, in large part because of our schooling in the liturgical and sacramental life of the Anglican church.

In sum, my own Canterbury Trail marked a pilgrimage to recover holiness, catholicity, apostolicity, authority. Michael was right: college evangelicals become Episcopalians because they seek visible shape to their confessed membership in "the one true holy catholic and apostolic church."

10.

Isabel Anders

"*Batter my heart, three-person'd God*
. . .
Your force, to breake, blowe, burn and
make me new . . ."

These lines from one of John Donne's *Holy Sonnets* hit me between the eyes the first time I encountered them in my text. I had come to Wheaton College with a vague intention of majoring in English literature and to plan for a writing career someday. There must have been divine providence in my registering for a class in seventeenth-century English literature. Reading John Donne and the other Anglican divines, I felt closer to finding an answer to one of my biggest questions in life: Is it possible to talk about God boldly, freshly—to know his impact in my life dramatically, unmistakably?

To me, Donne's words were like a prayer I was much too timid to express and incapable of verbalizing: "Invade my life, Lord—shattering all else." But this Anglican poet spoke with poetic, theological impact—and a passion and intellect I had never before seen connected with a personal faith.

I had come to college hoping that someday I myself would write something about God. Having been raised in a godly and serious Christian family, my questions were not, "Does God exist?" or "Am I connected to him?" but "*How* is my life in him to be expressed?"

I was thankful for a Christian home in which the Bible was taken seriously, in which personal faith in Christ was considered the beginning point for true life. The Bible teaching and memorization of my early years had largely shaped my vocational aspirations as well as my spiritual life to that point.

But I was seeking answers to nagging questions, some defendable philosophical structure to balance or supplement what seemed to me the rather hazy religious terminology I had grown up with. I have no quarrel with people who remain in fundamentalist churches and are happy with its terminology, forms of worship, and approaches to Christian living. But the doctrinal training of those early years had in some ways confused me, left me unsure, and sent me upon a long, hard search for authenticity. I wanted to remain true to the gospel I believed in without having to follow a simplistic approach to witnessing, settle for hackneyed expressions of faith, or limit my cultural experience to those who thought just as I did.

The biggest problem to me, I realize now, was a feeling of separation from the rest of the Christian world (not to mention the world in general). My home church seemed to believe that there were so few other "saved" people that, theoretically, they would have to find *us* and join up to be really *in,* to be part of a "New Testament" church.

I'm embarrassed to admit that when I got to college I didn't think anyone but those in my denomination qualified as *real* Christians. Did "one way in Christ" have to mean the one way we did it back home? I had to discard not only this thinking, but the attitude that automatically excluded people on first encounter, unless they could prove by their words that they were A-OK, in the fold. I was naively unaware of the arrogance that had been bred into me by this kind of thinking. I had adopted this attitude under the intention of obedience to church authority.

Yet I was troubled inside. I was constantly asking questions in my mind that didn't seem to be raised by the other people in my church. How does one account for the wildness and unfathomable variety in the world with bland, reduced language about faith? Often I was unable to formulate my heart's questions, yet

I realized that the style or expression of faith that those around me practiced happily left me half-empty.

I welcomed the academic standards of Wheaton, the rigors of study and research—exposure to the breadth of thoughts and ideas recorded by men and women with minds much greater than mine. I wanted to know more of life and grasp it whole, but not to surrender the childhood faith that was to me an inner fire, the center of my understanding of who I was before God. The question was not the faith itself, but the *expression* of that faith.

I never had great problems with my church's maxims of no drinking, smoking, or card playing. Dancing didn't appeal to me as I was too shy. But it *was* truly embarrassing when a fellow high school student once asked me what *else* I couldn't do. "Are you allowed to listen to the radio?" he asked me innocently.

I didn't like being identified negatively by what I *didn't* do. I didn't feel credible to the rest of the world, and for some reason that mattered to me very early. I wanted to talk in a language that was understandable to people "outside" because they were a part of my world too. I felt I had something positive inside to offer, but I was mostly inarticulate about it—silenced by my confusion and my guilt over not being "content," as Christians were supposed to be.

Most difficult was the expectation that I would have to go up to total strangers and "witness" or pass out tracts with a smile in order to convert someone on the spot to our "way." It was like being a salesman—not at all something I would choose to be. Yet I remember going out with a "team" to knock on doors in other north suburban Chicago homes and to give out flyers for Vacation Bible School, with the possibility of witnessing to people right there on their doorstep. I actually don't remember doing more than "selling" the person on our church and VBS.

But looking back, I'm still amazed that the command to "go into all the world" and be witnesses was so compelling that I was able to overcome my shyness and face unchurched strangers and be a witness. Perhaps some good did come out of that obedience, as bringing children to church can be a way of reaching whole families. And at my church they were able to find Christ, and a Christlike spirit in many of the people. Yet I was to find increasingly that this was not the branch of the Christian family tree in which I could best serve.

In college I even tried going out with Campus Crusade for Christ on outings to secular campuses, blitzing dorms with witnessing. And I remember at least one girl saying she would accept Christ on the spot. This was supposed to register her name in heaven—and I was being used. But I didn't really feel the elation or confidence about that that I was supposed to. I was high on the joy and camaraderie I felt with other witnesses, of being part of a mission but it didn't last. I still had too many questions of my own.

Ironically, I had never exactly had a "conversion" experience myself. I had grown up believing what I was told about Jesus and feeling accepted, praying in my private world and with my parents. For the first four years of grade school I had attended a Lutheran school, and there received some training in catechism, Scripture memorization, and old Lutheran hymns. It was during one of our opening sessions in the basement before classes, that I remember quietly receiving the assurance that Jesus was in my heart and that it was settled—I belonged to him. There was no appeal that day (or ever) for an evangelical kind of conversion or turning around (at age seven I didn't have much glaring sin to dramatically turn from). Yet I was aware that I wasn't good on my own, and that Christ made it all right with God for me to be accepted. From that time, I never had any real doubts that I was a Christian.

I truly wanted to live for the Lord; but I did not tell a soul. I kept it between me and God. My parents were not yet in the fundamentalist church, though my mother had had a fundamentalist upbringing. My father was dutifully attending the Lutheran church next to the school more or less regularly so that I could remain a student in good standing.

When my mother found a local fundamentalist church she preferred, we began going there. I had been baptized Lutheran as a baby, but I found that this church put its emphasis on adult decision-making and baptism, and clearly vocalizing your personal belief. My father at first resisted this change in churches, and especially rebaptism, but he gave in and became a hard-line convert. He and I were baptized together and joined the church when I was eleven. One thing I remember is everyone treated me as though I had suddenly chosen to change my life, turn around, be converted. But I knew inside that it wasn't quite true. I felt I had belonged to Jesus for years—and I had. What had been private was being made public, and the commitment *did* mean something to me. But I couldn't say what, at the time, so I went along silently. But, I wondered, why did every individual's salvation story have to fit the same exact description? My own didn't; yet I was expected to witness to others as though that were the norm, and I hadn't even experienced it. A nagging fear for the integrity of my witness was growing in me.

I was expected to be a witness by urging people to be "saved" and "born again," but even then I realized that the coded meaning behind those acceptable biblical phrases was, "you must have a conversion experience such as I have had" and "become the kind of Christian we say you need to be." The words themselves may have been all right, but they were in the wrong setting, or without adequate explanation or aptness, not words always "fitly spoken."

I wanted to be faithful to Christ, but I felt my opportunity would come about in another way. So I began early to pray for a language, a wider vision, a way of seeing and dialoguing with others that did not exclude them unless they chose to exclude *themselves* from Christ.

I remember being taught with flannelgraph and chalkboard, many Sunday school stories. Unfortunately, the medium can become the message in subtle ways to children. It is easy even now to think of Abraham and Isaac first as colored-paper figures with flannel backs! I don't know how we can expect most amateur teachers to get around simplistic Bible story retelling in order to emphasize the fullness and connectedness of the ongoing biblical story of God's dealing with mankind. It took me years of caring and searching to find out what relevance such stories had to my life. I am thankful at least that I am not biblically illiterate, that I held onto my Christian tradition, and that I could start at another point to search for deeper levels of meaning for my own life. More than anything else, the Book of Psalms (which my father always stressed and has read from every day of his life) helped me to see *myself* as crying out to God, somehow connected to this story of God's acts in history.

Otherwise, it was easy to see Old Testament figures, especially, as almost another breed of human, to whom God spoke in ways he *never* could be expected to speak to us—in fire and cloud and still, small voice, in miracles and written testament (which was now closed, finished—as we were in a new dispensation). But the heart cries of the psalmist helped to bridge this gap; I could cry out to God in my immediate situation and he would answer, though only in the still, small voice.

I know now what I was longing for—some expression of faith with more credibility in my situation, not sentimentality, to help me cut through the various data: the stories, the prayers, the gospel songs. Where was freshness of expression? Did it have to be only in the secular world? I longed for some awe toward the holy things of God . . . for some word of the *transcendence* and *immanence* of God (words I never heard until college) that would have helped me make sense of it all. I saw even then the reality of God's presence in the world. He was very real in my heart and I believed that he was also in heaven. What I needed was the word *paradox.*

I desired more complexity, not to annul or obscure the gospel, but to begin to account for all the varieties and modes of people and experiences that cropped up in everyday life. I longed to be able to say, in a much more sophisticated mode than I could yet imagine, "That is life, there is a givenness about it, and theology can accommodate its givenness without being washed away or made to look silly."

Looking back, I always hated to be copied by friends, in dress or words or other choices. I was told it was the highest compliment to be imitated, but I couldn't help thinking, "Why does she have to buy a dress just like mine?" or when parroted by someone, "But I said that first!" I guess the desire to be original in some way, to make a mark as an individual, to go on record as having said something a certain way, was a desire to be creative, eventually to be a writer. And in my faith I was also seeking creativity. I wanted to keep one foot on home base theologically, but to reach out with the other foot at least—like one of Donne's compasses, making a circle around a given point, enclosing the boundaries of what I could say about my faith and still be orthodox (another word I never heard until college).

The biggest expansion of my boundaries was to come when I arrived at Wheaton College. I wanted the high academic standards the college could offer, and the idea of being able to study various disciplines with a Christian perspective was immensely appealing. What surprised me was that, unlike my church, Wheaton did not teach me *what* to think, but rather *how* to think. As soon as I adjusted to that, it was like putting a hungry person before a full table. Everywhere I looked, there were ideas to be grasped, taken in, and digested over a period of time. And there were the checks and balances of the more developed minds of writers, leaders, and professors to guide me.

Other students may have complained about chapel, but to me the mere size of the gathering, the awe of silence and meditation, the music of worship I found there were greatly to be desired in a hectic life of rushing here and there. I eagerly looked forward to what speakers could do to help me piece together parts of the puzzle. Not all of them helped, of course, but I was gradually developing an open mind, something I had not been taught in my fundamentalist background.

During college my struggle was mostly internal. I stayed a member of my home church and was loyal to what I could affirm in my inherited tradition. I even went home many weekends to teach Sunday school. There was still enough to feed me in a church where the Bible was preached and people welcomed me. But the break was bound to come as inner growth ached for outer expression, and as I grew bolder in articulating my faith.

I thirsted for language that expressed and reflected my own journey. But I found I had to go outside my tradition into the broader catholic literature of spirituality to find it. Gradually I learned and adopted language that was orthodox and biblical, but that gave me variety of expression about my faith. It was clear to me that the style as well as the content matters, and that the way we present our lives to others determines whether we will have legitimate "takers" for our message.

I wondered how to express my journey of faith in the world with dignity and beauty of expression. To do less seemed to be to offer God a lesser sacrifice. But the mode of expression also had to be one that allowed the listener integrity, a style that was filled with charity and true compassion. The desire to be more creative and authentic edged me farther and farther from the fundamentalist circles.

Because life in my church was geared to getting everyone to make a one-time decision for Christ, other levels of growth, understanding, struggle, doubt, and certainly paradox in life were virtually unmentioned. My own life in Christ had been more like a pot slowly boiling and gathering steam, rather than a conversion fire quickly lit and instantly visible. Hadn't anyone else had a similar experience, I wondered? Yet Christ was central to these people and to me, so this bridge held me a while longer.

As a literature major I could justify reading widely and often in all kinds of literature, and I found that when an author from another culture, such as Dostoevsky in Russian Orthodox tradition, spoke beautifully and passionately of the struggles of a soul, I was moved and assured of a wider experience of Christ in those beyond my cultural background. I could enter into and celebrate the joy of fellowship with the saints in many times and places. This helped to keep me in the fold.

I was not much attracted to the literature of existential despair and chaos, as I felt I had enough of that in my own inner struggle and didn't care to wallow in it. Not having had a classical education with the firm boundaries of logic and balance I longed for, I was hungry for order amid freshness in the literature I read. I found a system of hierarchy and order in Shakespeare most appealing—an assumption of heavenly forces paralleling the earthly, of right and wrong; yet a poetic, nonmoralistic expression of these forces in the world.

When I first came to Wheaton I had never heard of C. S. Lewis, but I was soon to discover his logic and clear insight which would be my main apologetic guide through this period of genuine searching for a credible Christianity. I wanted what Lewis called *Mere Christianity*; it cut across denominational and partisan lines, and clearly honored Christ. So I was learning to be a mere Christian too, while searching for a denominational home.

After graduation from college, my parents sent me on a three-week tour of the British Isles, where I got to visit the birthplaces, museums, and graves of many of the poets I loved. I also attended several Anglican worship services: at St. Mary the Virgin Church in Oxford, where C. S. Lewis had preached his famous sermon, "The Weight of Glory"; and morning prayer at Canterbury Cathedral.

I was quite unaware of the ongoing Anglican tradition in my own country—the Episcopal church. And so the division between my worship and intellectual life continued after I returned home.

That summer I began my first job after college at an evangelical publishing firm. It was natural and relatively easy for me to think in terms of teaching and promoting Christian truth, and I found that my years in church work, a knowledge of the Bible, and an ability to think in logical steps helped me to do my job and to grow personally as well. This immersion in the broader evangelical world was satisfying, as it gave me a more ecumenical spirit of understanding and helped to unite me in purpose and work with fellow Christians. The evangelical associations of my editorial career, and many related friendships, have nurtured me through the years.

During these years of work, I worshiped with a small group of other post-college people that always met in someone's living room. We had basically a write-your-own-liturgy policy, with someone giving an inspirational talk, followed by singing to guitar accompaniment. We all sat on the floor and wore blue jeans in those mid-1970s; and if we weren't sure what we were about as a "church," we at least knew we didn't really belong anywhere else at that point.

To go from that very "low" (on the floor) church experience to the high church liturgy of St. Barnabas' Episcopal Church in Glen Ellyn, Illinois, was quite a shock. I had been invited by a friend and colleague, also from an evangelical background, who had shared my love of Anglican and Catholic literature. I immediately discovered many things in the liturgy to which I *could* relate, similarities to the Anglican services I had attended in England. But most importantly, I discovered a whole tradition of worship that had been going on for centuries expressed, in language—about and directed toward God—which had been refined and kept fresh and vital. The service had a dignity and awe that fed my spirit. I also found a thinking community I could relate to; people who admitted to similar questions and searching and a desire to keep learning. The sermons or homilies delivered by the vicar were so fine that you wanted a transcript to take home and read again (which he sometimes provided when asked). In the Inquirers' Class and other small group meetings at the church, he helped searchers such as myself to integrate our biblical learning and liturgical worship with understanding and clarity.

So, as it turned out, it was not primarily in intellectual pursuit nor philosophical structure that I was to find answers to the deepest questions with which I had been struggling. It was rather *in the Anglican tradition of worship* that my faith and its proper expression were to come together naturally.

I was confirmed in the Episcopal Church, in fear and trembling, in October 1976. I found that, because I had kept much of my spiritual journey inside myself, and because it had been reflected in unobtrusive ways in my life, it was difficult to explain to my parents and to some friends how I had come to this point and what adult confirmation meant to me. But I struggled to share as much as I could with them, realizing that to many evangelicals the Episcopal church meant nothing except controversial headlines on issues of homosexuality, women priests, Bishop Pike's story, and all kinds of things for which I didn't feel I had to have answers.

For me, joining the church was a personal step of dedication to service, along with a very human army of saints, in a tradition I had entered gradually but enthusiastically. I wanted to take up my adult responsibility in a local congregation and put my efforts there, rather than not use them or give up on finding a "perfect" church. It was important at that time for me to make a concrete commitment, to realize that no perfect church exists (if it did, it would never accept me). But this church was a respected and valid corner of the church in which I found I could serve with my own gifts and limitations, which is all one can do.

In membership I would cease to be a bystander and would cast my lot with others of varying circumstances, for better or worse. The church asks of me that I share my journey; this is something I can offer, as can any believer. When I took this step of commitment, God's blessing was confirmed to me again and again by the opening of avenues for my talents and inclinations to serve. I realized soberly that when you join an organized church body, you can no longer complain about "the church" as something other than yourself. You are part and parcel of the whole.

The Anglican tradition suited my own sensibilities, in that I found a dignity and reverence for the things of God, a care for language and learning, an awareness of history and also an openness to new leading of the Holy Spirit in our day. Martin Thornton in his book *English Spirituality* speaks of the spiritual tradition of the church as "sane, wise, ancient, modern, sound, and simple; with roots in the New Testament and the Fathers . . . with its golden periods and its full quota of saints and doctors . . . ."

I also found in my church a belief in the primacy of Christ and the Scriptures, such that, with the complement of biblical preaching, the liturgy becomes a full expression of our devotion to God, our "reasonable service." This for me means *something I can do.* I can identify myself with other believers in ongoing worship.

I discovered that the readings from Scripture itself, within the context of liturgy, had new meaning for me. I listened more carefully to the spoken words, as they were given the chance to stand alone, not to be dissected or interpreted immediately. Scripture describes itself, in Proverbs 25:11: "A word fitly spoken is like apples of gold in a setting of silver." In other words, the frame or setting that surrounds the proclamation of the Word can add or detract.

In the Episcopal church I found that the reverence and deliberate attention given to Scripture readings—from the Old Testament, a Psalm, a New Testament passage, and finally, the Gospel—brought a new focus to my understanding. It was sometimes easy in my former tradition to gloss over the actual wording of the passage and skip to the interpretation accepted by the group—the "message." Yet I had learned as a student of literature that a coded message is not the same as the literature itself. Cliff's Notes cannot substitute for the work.

I realize that my experience is the exact opposite of some who discover evangelical preaching for the first time. For these people, the Word as interpreted by the preacher suddenly *takes on* meaning. I rejoice in this, and am thankful that God uses many means to awaken people to his lively Word. But since my problem had been one of oversaturation in interpretation, the experience of Scripture in the Episcopal church was one way he awakened me.

The whole issue of proclaiming our faith, of witnessing, also has gradually become resolved for me in the context of the Episcopal church. As I began to understand more of the corporate nature of the church and how my own salvation story related to the whole, as a variation on God's work in many lives, I became more confident and found more accurate language to speak of it. I discovered that I have the gift of encouraging people in their walk with Christ, of directing others to Scripture and other sources of spiritual instruction, and of sharing some of my own history of struggle for the expression and life of faith.

I find that it is natural to talk about God and my church experience with people I meet in various circumstances, such as with a scientist I once sat next to on a plane flight, who said he was an agnostic, but his wife was practicing Bahaism. I do not know what kind of influence I may have had; but when spiritual topics come naturally into a conversation, I can at least speak with conviction of my own faith and practice in the context of the church. I can share what Christ means to me, and interact with the person's questions and doubts, and even anger, as the Spirit gives me courage and the words to say. Perhaps I have now gained enough life experience to speak with more credibility from my tradition and my faith, in words that have become my own, whether they are exact Scripture quotations or not. I have reached a more satisfactory level of integration of faith in my own life story, such that I do not feel *forced* to speak of Christ, under fear of disobedience; but rather feel that I cannot adequately share myself if I keep my Christianity hidden or unexpressed.

I am glad to speak of my church and its importance to me. I find in the spirit of Anglican preaching a model for approaching others for Christ positively—to begin at whatever point the person is able to affirm and build from there. In my experience, this preaching has been centered on Christ, what is freely given to us through his salvation, and can grow toward claiming the fullness of life in him. When people come to worship Christ and say they want to be part of the body, they are encouraged and taught rather than grilled and categorized. There is an acceptance of people at many levels of seeking, service, and commitment, that gives the body its flavor of variety and its many opportunities for continued witness, encouragement, and strengthening within the body. No one has it "made." We are all learners together;

and even if we once had certain steps of obedience down pat, we always need to be reminded of them again. We are a body, not of perfect Christians, but of people always needing Christ to fill us; and worship provides that opportunity to "refuel" on an ongoing basis.

I have discovered that the Book of Common Prayer and the seasons of the church calendar that we follow, are often envied by other denominations, who sometimes look to our forms, at least for their wedding services. To me the prayer book offers much variety as well as the familiar patterns of response we can count on. The readings for each Sunday are provided on a three-year cycle, which covers most of the Bible in those three years, including Old and New Testament readings, Psalms, and Gospel each Sunday. This allows the preacher or homilist a variety of themes and connections to discover in Scripture and build on in his message. There is also a daily reading schedule of Scripture provided through the Christian year.

Since we celebrate communion each Sunday (Eucharist itself means the giving of thanks), there is a spirit of thanksgiving around the Lord's Table that offers us a chance both to receive and to give back to God. In partaking, we rededicate ourselves to his service and trust our lives to his care for the coming week.

The same year that I was confirmed in the Episcopal church, I also began work at Tyndale House Publishers in Wheaton, Illinois, as a book editor. Tyndale is a nondenominational evangelical publisher, and is large and comprehensive enough to publish books (80 to 100 a year) from various Christian points of view.

My colleagues at Tyndale come from various denominations themselves, and several of them came to my confirmation to support my decision and rejoice with me in that commitment to the church of my choice. There is an atmosphere of dialogue and support among my colleagues that has made my years at Tyndale a large area of support in my personal life, as well as an opportunity to work toward a common purpose.

In June 1982 I was appointed by the Bishop of Chicago to serve on the diocesan Advisory Commission on Communications, as a representative working in religious print media. On the first day of the commission's reorganization, I met the newly appointed chairman, the Rev. John R. Throop.

John and I began conversing after the meeting, and I told him the areas to which I thought I could contribute at a later date, as a writer interested in Anglican heritage.

John had grown up Roman Catholic and had had a conversion experience during his first year of college in California, in which his life became redirected around a personal relationship with Jesus Christ. He had gone far from family and familiar surroundings in Chicago to "find himself" but had instead found Christ. He began the struggle to integrate his new understanding with his Catholic upbringing, in which he had always attended church, expressed his belief in God, and been serious about life. But he was experiencing a call to more commitment, and eventually to the ministry—which would demand years of preparation and service.

Both of us had had difficulty in explaining to our parents our adult choice of a church tradition different from the one in which we had grown up. He had tried to bring his family along as far as possible with him, to help them understand his journey and choice of the Episcopal church, as I had with my Baptist parents.

As our relationship with each other developed steadily I began to see how the Lord was bringing many parts of my diverse experience together to give me the opportunity of parish ministry along with this man whom I respected and could support in love and shared service. Through prayer and discussion and a joyful unfolding of the circumstances, we became engaged and began to plan our wedding for June of 1983.

Shortly after our honeymoon, John was called by the search committee of Church of the Mediator in Chicago. In September we found ourselves moving into a large Georgian rectory on the southwest side of Chicago, to begin our work together in a new setting.

I have had to begin thinking deeply and practically about my role in the parish, now that I am in a more clearly defined role in relation to the church. I see myself not as an assistant minister, but as wife, companion, and supporter of my husband's work. I am growing in understanding of the many aspects of his ministry.

And I found that in narrowing down—choosing one church denomination, one vocation, one life—there is, paradoxically, a broadening of perspective, an ability to embrace more and more of life, and to be thankful for it. There is in the church the possibility of fellowship that makes the ups and downs of life bearable.

And so, through many years of searching, I now find myself deeply committed to a life of service with my husband—no more and no less important than many other ministries—but with clear marching orders for now, and a fulfillment beyond my imagination when I first saw those words, "Batter my heart . . . ."

The battering and the healing have been one.

11.

David and LaVonne Neff

On March 24, 1968, David Neff and LaVonne Pease were married in the La Sierra, California, Seventh-day Adventist Church. David wanted to have a communion service as part of the ceremony, so LaVonne broached the idea with her father, the officiating minister. "I can understand why you might want that," he said. (LaVonne's father is always tactful.) "But I'm afraid it would be misunderstood. It just looks too Catholic." David and LaVonne dropped the idea.

On October 10, 1982, LaVonne and David were confirmed at St. Barnabas Episcopal Church, Glen Ellyn, Illinois. The ceremony seemed pretty Catholic. Their parents were not present.

***

A journey always has a starting point as well as a destination. It is hard to explain our pilgrimage to Canterbury without saying something about our point of departure.

Life for us began in the Seventh-day Adventist Church—a religion that emphasizes its unique calling to be the church of Jesus Christ in our time. "The remnant church of Bible prophecy," they call it. Although our Adventist elders taught us that there were sincere and devout Christians in all Christian denominations, they also stressed that someday, not far off, the important spiritual truths taught by Seventh-day Adventism would become clear to everyone. In that day, they said, all the "honest-in-heart" would step forward and declare themselves for the seventh-day Sabbath and the other distinctive Adventist doctrines.

David: Adventism broadened its outlook during my childhood. While giving lip service to its calling to be the "remnant church," church leaders sought recognition by the evangelical community as one evangelical denomination among many. The message was mixed—Adventism was both the "remnant church of Bible prophecy" and just one more evangelical church with some contributions it could make to the larger community.

My father wanted it both ways. He believed in the special doctrines and practices of the Adventist church and wanted me to share his commitment. He also believed that other Christians were not enemies, but brothers, and he wanted me to share his openness.

One way he tried to teach me about other Christians was to encourage me to join the paid boy choir at the Episcopal church that sat, gray, gothic, and forbidding only blocks from our white clapboard Adventist church/schoolhouse. As a boy, Dad had earned pocket money singing in an Episcopal boy choir. He had earned more than the few pennies they paid the boys: he had earned an appreciation for good church music and creedal orthodoxy as well.

I dug in my heels and refused to sell my soul to those near-Catholics who used incense, knelt for communion, and made the sign of the cross. I did, however, file Dad's lesson away for future reference.

LaVonne: Like David, I received a mixed message about the Adventist church. My father a college president, seminary professor, and writer was a leader in the movement toward Evangelicalism. Respectability in the eyes of other Christians was important to my family.

At the same time, church and school teachings left no doubt in my mind. The Seventh-day Adventist church was God's one true church. All the rest were second-class at best. One day during Bible class when I was twelve years old, the thought flew through my mind: "Maybe God, who knows the end from the beginning, knows that someday I will leave the Adventist church." I quickly banished the thought. It was too horrible to imagine.

The summer I turned seventeen my parents and I lived in England while my father taught a class in worship at a Seventh-day Adventist seminary. Every Sunday we went to some city or another where, inevitably, at least two renowned preachers were holding forth. One Sunday we heard John Stott in the morning and David Martyn Lloyd-Jones in the evening. My parents loved every minute of it. "If anyone gets to heaven, surely Dr. Stott will," my mother said. I liked him too, but I wondered why the services had to be so long.

After three weeks of touring interspersed with two-hour-long church services replete with at least nine psalms and thirty-one Gloria Patris each, I flatly refused to go anywhere with my parents on a Sunday. My introduction to Anglicanism was not calculated to make me want to switch.

David: Childhood certainty about the Adventist church gave way to a more tentative approach when I took a college major in theology. It became evident that not everything the Adventist church had taught me was true. My seminary education left me yet less sure.

Why then did I stay? Why was I ordained an Adventist minister? I knew Adventism as my spiritual home. And at the same time that I discovered the loopholes in the doctrinal logic, I also discovered something about the nature of the church.

The church is seen, with Adventist eyes, as an organization supported by a structure of beliefs. What you believe is what determines whether or not you are a member of the church. More detailed and more uniform belief is the goal of Adventist preaching. The goal of Adventist Evangelism is to change religious opinions.

But my biblical studies in Adventist schools taught me that the church is more an organism than an organization. Shared beliefs were important to the organism, but so were worship and service and mutual caring. My shift in understanding the nature of the church allowed me to stay in Adventism even after I learned that I could never buy its total package of beliefs.

LaVonne: I have always needed to believe wholeheartedly in what I'm doing. This applies to my work, my church affiliation, and my personal relationships. Life would be much easier if I could take it less seriously, but that's not my gift.

For years I believed wholeheartedly that the Seventh-day Adventist church was God's one true church. I believed the church's biblical and historical interpretations, as well as its theological statements and ethical norms. I pushed aside certain recurring problems, such as the fact that I found Adventist worship services unhelpful and boring, and the more important fact that I felt insecure about my own salvation.

I began to question Adventist beliefs when, in the early '70s, a perfectionistic group of church leaders began teaching that the saved person is eventually enabled to live without sinning. I knew this bore no resemblance to my own experience, and I ascertained that it was not biblical, but I could not avoid seeing the strong perfectionistic strain in early Adventist writings.

While checking up on Adventist soteriology, I concluded that their eschatology was questionable. This led me to look into the Adventist historical interpretation that for decades has persuaded the faithful to keep a seventh-day Sabbath. I was amazed to learn that it too is shaky at best.

I need to believe in what I'm doing. And being a religion teacher, writer, and pastor's wife in a church whose soteriology, eschatology, and historical interpretation were all unacceptable to me quickly became a severe problem.

David: I was evangelical, and I was Adventist. One label for my thoughts, the other for my subculture. But the time came when I could no longer have it both ways. Pharaohs arose who knew not the desire to be called evangelical. Prophets spoke forth who knew no other desire. The resulting conflict drew the lines between the evangelical Adventists and the traditional, the *real,* Adventists.

I cast my lot with the evangelicals. But I could not cast that lot without struggle. The impetus for the struggle came from LaVonne. For reasons whose depth I never felt, she suffered acute discomfort at living as a leader and a leader's wife in a strict and coercive religious subculture whose basic beliefs she could not affirm. LaVonne urged me to find another way to make a living so that she could at least take a vacation from her influential role as a writer and teacher in Adventism. *Urge* is perhaps too mild a word to represent the frequency and force with which I felt her request.

LaVonne: David has always said that he's like Erasmus and I'm like Luther. I could see no possible way to stay in, much less represent, a church whose dominant symbols and major doctrines were no longer mine. David could see no reason not to stay in such a church and believe whatever he wished. I argued for honesty, he for commitment. But for several years nothing changed except our frustration level. It took an event in the Adventist church to move us to resolution.

David: Commitment is and has always been one of the chief gods in my pantheon. Was I not called to the ministry of the gospel? I asked myself. Am I not best suited by upbringing and education to minister that gospel within the context of the Adventist church? What really was the commitment I made to the Adventist church on the day of my ordination? How should the commitments I made to LaVonne on the day of our marriage control my vocational decisions now?

I was seriously tortured by my conflict of commitments when I received news that a ministerial colleague in California (a former Anglican turned Adventist) had plunged himself into the midst of a heresy trial for publicly espousing views that we had privately discussed the year before. Des Ford was still a loyal Adventist struggling to harmonize the truth he understood with the traditions of the elders. I knew then that the outcome of Des's heresy trial would be a message for me. I made my pact with God that if there was to be room for me in the Adventist church, he would make room for Des also. He didn't.

Throughout the period of my struggles, I looked to my fellow clergy in Walla Walla, Washington, for support and understanding. A dozen or so of us clergy gathered each Tuesday morning to consume a dozen or two doughnuts and to discuss the lectionary readings for the following Sunday. The group sessions built clergy camaraderie and, I hope, improved our preaching.

Fr. Ernie Campbell, rector of St. Paul's Episcopal Church, seemed to be one of the more sensitive and understanding members of the group. I thought he could understand both my conflicts and the need to keep quiet about them. So I made a date to talk to Ernie.

Ernie offered me tea as we settled down to talk. He explained that time was limited because he needed to prepare for a vestry meeting in which the factions of his congregation were to argue the pros and cons of holding folk masses once a month for the benefit of the local cursillo (a kind of study course) alumni. Time was too short that day, and other talks followed.

From our talks—or perhaps just from hanging around the worship services at St. Paul's—I came to realize that Ernie and my Episcopal friends understood the church in a way that was significantly different from my Adventist-colored ecclesiology. To my Adventist friends, the church was a community of people built around a common doctrinal commitment. The essence of being Adventist did not lie half so much in worshiping God on Saturday morning as it did in *believing* that Saturday morning was the right time for worship. To my Episcopal friends, the church was a community built around a common worship commitment. They were able to tolerate a fair amount of difference in religious beliefs, but the 1979 revision of their prayer book precipitated a major religious crisis for many of them. Of course, my Adventist community believed that proper worship was important, and the folk at St. Paul's believed that orthodox doctrine was essential. But the mainspring of community identity was different.

And then the light dawned. I had made a commitment to lead a worshiping community—but my church understood itself primarily as a believing community. Somehow the Adventist church and I had misunderstood the basic terms of the contract to which we were parties at my ordination. I now realized that I could never fulfill my role as a worship leader within Adventism as long as I held beliefs that conflicted with parts of its total package.

Whether that was sufficient justification for breaking my commitment or not, I shall leave for you to judge. However, I now felt free to follow wholeheartedly my other big commitment, the spiritual health of the woman I loved.

LaVonne: When I concluded that I could no longer agree with the teachings of my church, I no longer felt obligated to stay with it. When David concluded that his commitment to God differed from the commitment the church expected him to fulfill, he felt free to leave. But our mental separation from the church did not in itself make leaving possible. We had to find a way to support ourselves, and we had to deal with strong ties of family and friendship.

Over the course of two years, David looked at several possibilities. He visited with the Episcopal bishop of Spokane, but found that what they really needed were non-stipendiary clergy—not a very good way to finance a major life change. Inter-Varsity Christian Fellowship asked him to be the campus staff person at a Nevada university. A political candidate wanted him to manage his campaign. A large Presbyterian church looked at him as a candidate to be their minister to college students. Nothing seemed to fit.

I tried to hide from my parents both our feelings about the Adventist church and our search for other employment. I once offered the opinion that one's commitment to God should transcend one's commitment to a denomination. My father responded, "No matter what the Adventist church does, I will always be a loyal member." I did not think he would understand our increasing discomfort.

In the spring of 1981, InterVarsity Press asked David to be assistant editor of *HIS* magazine. He flew to Illinois, liked what he saw, and accepted the job.

We decided that it fit for several reasons. First, since IVP is Christian, we would have fellowship while we severed old denominational ties, put friendships at risk, and looked for a new church. Second, since it is interdenominational, our accepting the job would not need to be interpreted as leaving the Adventist denomination. David's church members would not have to think of him as an apostate; he could be spared much interrogation and accusation. Third, editorial work has different pressures from pastoral work. David would be able to give more attention to planning his own future if, for a time, he did not have to deal with everyone else's problems too. And, not least important, we have always respected InterVarsity Press and *HIS*.

My parents were upset and hurt that we had not discussed the move with them before making the decision. They were also confused about how to relate to us, we later learned. Were we backslidden Adventists who needed to be reclaimed? Were we going through some sort of adolescent rebellion? Or were we loyal Adventists on temporary leave? They decided to act as if the latter were true.

We moved to Illinois in June 1981, transferring our church membership to an Adventist congregation that we never attended. We were confirmed into the Episcopal church in October 1982. Those sixteen months were both exciting and painful.

David: When we arrived in Illinois, we set about searching for housing, new friends, and a church. One Presbyterian church we attended was friendly enough, but the contemporary prayers were uncomfortably trendy sounding. The next Presbyterian church we attended was mirthless. (We sang the "Old Hundredth" the first Sunday we visited there—how Reformed can you get? And I noticed that the words of the hymn had been changed from the old "Him serve with mirth, his praise forthtell" to "Him serve with fear. . . . ")

Several of our fellow employees at InterVarsity Press were Episcopalians. That made it thinkable for us seriously to consider several of the local Episcopal churches. One parish especially excited us—the people were interesting, the liturgy was high, the singing was enthusiastic, the architecture emphasized both mystery and community. But we weren't quite ready to commit ourselves to such an Anglo-Catholic, liturgical style. It was one thing to be a visitor at an Episcopal service and to mimic the motions. That was play. But to *be* an Episcopalian and bend the knee, make the sign of the cross, and smell the incense in earnest—that was another matter entirely.

We struggled with the liturgy and juggled the three books necessary to make it through the services at St. Barnabas, gamely giving it a try for several months. It didn't work. Our feelings of superiority surfaced whenever something appeared in the prayers or the sermon that made these Episcopalians seem like nominal Christians who might know their prayerbooks but probably didn't know their Scriptures.

God's Spirit reprimanded me twice during the liturgy. Once as I whispered the canon of the mass with the priest, I realized I didn't really mean the words "and at the last day bring us with all your saints into the joy of your eternal kingdom." I knew that I *should* mean those words. But I also felt that I had more spiritual knowledge than many of those kneeling around me. I didn't really want to share the joys of God's eternal kingdom with those particular people. Convicted of my spiritual pride, I saw that committing myself to the community prayers was a safeguard against elitism. So I learned to pray the prayers of the church in faith that God's Spirit would modify my will to match his purpose.

On another occasion we were chanting the creed and came to the phrase, "He descended into hell." I smugly thought of how that doctrine was based on a misreading of a probably corrupt text. The Spirit asked me who I thought I was. Not that I shouldn't hold that opinion. But that I should for that reason hold back from confessing the faith of the whole church. Even if the classic expressions of the church's faith are flawed, no Christian has the authority to decide as an individual what it means to be orthodox. Defining orthodoxy, I became convinced, was the business of the whole church.

Our friends were supportive of our interest in the Episcopal church. Our families were not. When I told my mother that we were attending the Episcopal church, she replied, with true sectarian horror, "Isn't that the church that's almost Catholic?" She told me she wasn't sleeping nights. She said she couldn't face her friends.

My father behaved better. One night on the telephone, Mother objected, "But we didn't raise you this way!" Dad said, "Oh, yes we did. We raised him to think for himself." Nevertheless, it was clear that Dad was pained and confused both by our decision to leave the Adventist church and by our interest in the Episcopal church.

LaVonne: I don't know if my parents reacted more strongly than David's or if I'm just more sensitive to parental reaction. I'm convinced now that I was unwise to tell them as little as possible of our changing directions. Though I said little, they suspected much. They probed, and I reacted with resentment and confusion.

Thanksgiving 1981 we hit bottom with my parents. The Sunday after Thanksgiving, we took them to St. Barnabas, thinking it would interest them like the Anglican services they had so relentlessly attended in England. It did not. Both were horrified, because this time we were participating and not just observing.

Mother rode home with me. "Your father had tears in his eyes

when you took communion," she said. "How can you like a
church that is so Catholic?" I, the eternal chicken, told her that
David liked it better than I did—true enough, but not fair or
honest under the circumstances.

My father rode home with David.

David: On the way home, LaVonne's father began, in his po-
lite but nervous manner, to tell us that the architecture, the
sanctuary lamp, and the worshipers' signs of reverence were all
signs of belief in the Real Presence in the bread and wine. I
reminded him that the mainstream Protestant Reformers continued to believe in the Real Presence, that Jesus' presence in the
sacrament was *not* one of the issues of the Reformation. And I
pointed out that even Adventists, with their Zwinglian understanding of communion, officially required that the consecrated
bread and wine be handled only by designated people and in
certain ways. By the time we got home, relationships had dete-
riorated almost beyond repair.

LaVonne: Maybe not almost beyond repair. For all the grief
our move has caused my parents, they would never repudiate us.
But for them, far more than for David's parents, the Adventist
church is their whole life. It cannot be separated from what they
do, think, or say in any area. Since we are now Episcopalians,
there is inevitable tension when we are together. The tension
would be there no matter what church we had chosen, but it is
probably greater because we chose a liturgical church.

In the course of studying, teaching, and writing about worship, my father has visited all types of church services. "There
are two kinds I don't think I'll ever be able to relate to," he told
me recently. "Charismatic services and liturgical services." For
him, the best definition of worship is the one offered by Ilion T.
Jones: "what a thinking man does as he approaches another
thinking being called God." If nonintellectual elements in-
trude—whether gestures like upraised arms and bended knee, or
equipment like liturgical vestments and incense, or beliefs like
the doctrine of the Real Presence or the desirability of speaking
in tongues—he grows uncomfortable. I think his discomfort is
caused by his background and personality type. He thinks it is
an early warning system against pagan excess. In any case, it's
not going to change.

David: I was the brash one of the team, willing fairly early to be confirmed in the Episcopal church. LaVonne was slower. A lot hinged on what each of us saw as the meaning of confirmation. Was it simply the formal process one went through in order to gain admission to the Episcopal church? Did it mean that we were now giving an adult witness to the promises we had made as children? Did it mean that our previous Christian initiation was incomplete just because a bishop was not involved? Did it mean we were making a lifetime commitment to a new denomination? Did it mean we were swearing fealty to a prince of the church?

I decided that for me confirmation meant the formal process of admission into the Episcopal church. In addition, it was a recognition of the historic episcopate—that the bishops were the historic preservers of the faith and that in their office they represented the whole church in its struggle to preserve and interpret "the faith once delivered to the saints." Sectarianism, the notion that a group or an individual who thinks he has truth that the rest of the church has forgotten or missed should separate from it, was now anathema to me.

I had been taught that the General Conference of the Seventh-day Adventist Church was God's highest authority on earth and that individuals should submit their understandings of Scripture to its judgment. (That kind of conciliar authority was awfully Catholic for a group that claimed to be the only pure Protestants.) Of course, the Adventists stood apart from the rest of Christ's church because they would not submit their idiosyncratic interpretations of Scripture and theology to the judgment of the larger church. To affirm the value of the historic episcopate and the church councils was no great leap for me, but simply the transfer of authority from one locus to another.

My confirmation was a choice in favor of the whole church rather than just a splinter of it. And my confirmation was a prayer in action and word for the unity of the church of Jesus Christ.

LaVonne: David's reasoning was quite persuasive—to my *mind.* But when I was in church, the memory of my parents' horror swept over me. When I was only visiting, I loved the high-church liturgy. Now that I might join, I was terrified. What if my grade school teachers had been right about Catholics? Would I imperil my salvation by worshiping with the aid of

smells, bells, and costumes? Could I pray in a church that referred to "The Blessed Virgin Mary"?

My mind was convinced months before my heart could follow. I could not decide on mind alone. Part of my problem with
the Adventist church had been that my heart was not truly involved in worship there. I needed to get heart, soul, strength,
and mind together before committing them to the Lord in any
new fashion.

In the meantime I attended church at least weekly, sometimes
more. I familiarized myself with the Book of Common Prayer. I
memorized the prayers and responses used every Sunday. No
longer did I have to juggle two hymn books, a prayer book, and
a bulletin at each service.

And then one Sunday it all came together. We were singing
the Gloria. I wasn't fumbling to follow the service or carrying on
an inner dialogue about what I was doing in a room with incense. Instead I was singing Glory to God in the highest. I was
worshiping with my heart and with my mind.

I went home and told David I was ready to be confirmed.

I do not want to give the impression that I think liturgical
worship is better than free-church worship, or that people in
free-church traditions are not worshiping with their hearts. I
have told my story, not someone else's. My parents worship
God with all their hearts, souls, and minds in the denomination
that left me empty. They are put together differently from me;
their religious needs are different and must be met by different
means.

I have a friend, raised in the Catholic church, who found that
the liturgy destroyed her religious experience. She now worships
God in a Bible church. Both of us have chosen to worship God
with our own hearts, souls, and minds, even though our approach has had to differ from that of our parents.

Intellectually, I need room to toss ideas about. I want to be
able to look at all sides of all questions, to try on many answers
before adopting one or throwing the whole lot out. When we
were shopping for a denomination I told David, "I don't want to
join a church that I agree with on all points. If I did, I'd never be
able to change my mind again." The Episcopal church errs on
the side of freedom and openness. It satisfies my intellectual
need to explore. It would not satisfy a person whose need is for

certainty and limits—and there is nothing wrong with such a person. The world needs people who play with ideas, and it also needs people who send down deep roots.

Spiritually, I need an environment that ushers me into God's presence and gives me time to drink it in. The predictable rhythm of the Episcopal service frees me to worship. I do not find God as easily in a service centered around a sermon; in most cases I liked the book better. In a free-church service, the confession or the creed or the Old Testament lesson may be left out. I miss these elements that lead me naturally to God. I am distracted by innovations. Other people are bored by the prayer book's regularity or offended by its repetitions which they find meaningless. The Christian world needs both kinds of worshipers. That is why the body of Christ has so many parts.

In this account, we have focused on our own experiences and our relationships with our parents. If we have left out the rest of our immediate family—our daughters, Molly and Heidi, who were ten and eight when we made the move—it is because the change seemed to affect them so little.

For two years before we moved to Illinois, the girls attended Adventist worship services on Saturday morning and Presbyterian Sunday school the next day. One summer they went to Vacation Church School at the Episcopal church in Walla Walla and learned about the major feasts of the church year. They simply had not been raised with a one-true-church mentality, so leaving the Adventist church to become Episcopalians was not earth-shaking to them.

They do worry about how to relate to their grandparents without offending them. One daughter is hesitant to be confirmed, because she has seen how hard it can be to get out of something once you're well into it. We hope that, as a result of what we have gone through with our own parents, we will be more willing than we might otherwise have been to let our daughters follow their own convictions, even if they are not convictions we share. Time will tell.

The Church
of the Future

12.

Sign of Renewal

---◆---

My experience in the church seems to suggest that the future of the church lies in the convergence of the evangelical and catholic traditions.

Reverend Robert McFarlane
Rector, St. Barnabas Episcopal Church
Glen Ellyn, Illinois

In 1983 I had the privilege of delivering the commencement homily at Seabury-Western Theological Seminary, a seminary of the Episcopal Church, located in Evanston, a beautiful suburb of Chicago. It was a regal commencement held in the context of a full service of worship, characterized by a sense of triumph and joy. The faces of the graduates together with family and friends who joined on this happy occasion were beaming with pride and a sense of accomplishment. The commencement, like all commencements, ended with a glorious recession followed by the immediate hub-bub of relatives and friends converging on the graduates with congratulations and best wishes. While all this was happening, I stood by a small rose garden soaking in the spring sun, watching the gleeful responses of all the people with a feeling of nostalgia, remembering my own commencements. A faculty member, seeing me alone and desiring to say something nice, walked up to me. In a friendly manner, he shook my hand firmly and said, "Good homily, much better than I expected." Not knowing how to take the last phrase I responded, "Well, what do you mean by that?" "Well, you know," he said smiling, "can any good thing come out of Wheaton?" And with a wave he turned on his heel and was lost in the crowd.

My reaction to his statement was not very positive to say the least. I felt put down, angry, and frustrated. After all, I thought, what does he know about Wheaton? I know Wheaton College; I know the administration, faculty, and students. I know them to be deeply dedicated Christians, honest scholars, and positive contributors to society. I'm proud to be a part of Wheaton and what it represents. Why should he put us down and treat us as inferior?

Then I began to reflect on other situations within evangelical communities—colleges, seminaries, and churches—where similar incidents had occurred. When I speak at one of these places someone will invariably ask me, "And where do you go to church?" I'm always straightforward and simply say, "I'm an Episcopalian." And then, as though to regain some credibility, I'll usually say, "But I did grow up as a Baptist." Now, while these evangelicals have never voiced the words, "Can any good thing come out of the Episcopal Church?" I've seen it in their eyes, heard it in their "Oh," and sensed it in their body language.

My recall of these instances did not lessen the sting of the faculty member's remark, but it did help me put it into context. The unhappy fact is that we all tend to live in our own spiritual ghettos. Our security is in things as we know them to be. And the thought that someone who lives in another spiritual tradition can also have a valid relationship with Christ is threatening to our own security. No one has a monopoly on bigotry and closedmindedness. We all wear blinders.

The question I want to address in this epilogue grows out of the comment made by the faculty member at the Seabury-Western commencement. Can we in liturgical churches and evangelicals learn something from each other and thus strengthen our own tradition? What does the liturgical tradition have to offer the evangelical community? What does the evangelical tradition have to offer the liturgical community?

The purpose of this book has been to explain why evangelicals are attracted to the liturgical tradition, especially the Episcopal church. But the issue is much broader than that. Evangelicals are returning to main-line denominations—to Methodist, Presbyterian, Lutheran, United Church of Christ, and Catholic churches. This book has been about that migration, and six reasons have been given for the trek into these churches—mystery, worship, sacraments, historical identity, ecumenical affirmation, and holistic spirituality. But evangelicals who come into these churches bring with them their evangelical roots, a heritage that has positive distinctions, experiences that can contribute to the spiritual life of the Episcopal community.

Another book could easily be written titled *Evangelical Contribution to Canterbury: What Evangelicals Bring to the Liturgical Tradition*. I would like, in the next few pages, to point out the strengths of the evangelical community, strengths which evangelicals bring into the liturgical church.

The word *evangelical* is a translation of the Greek word *euangelion* which means good news or gospel. Historically, it was first used by Erasmus in derision of the Lutherans; i.e., "these are those evangelicals who stress the gospel." Since the Reformation the term has been used to describe the movements of Christian

awakening and revival such as the evangelical revivals under
John Wesley and George Whitefield, or the evangelical awaken-
ings in America. This usage of the word gives a clue to the
central thrust, the heartbeat of evangelicalism. It is a movement
of renewal, a movement that calls for the experience of personal
faith and trust in Christ. What evangelicals bring into the liturgical tradition is a strong sense of personal faith, a deep abiding
peace that God in Christ has reconciled the world, has indeed
forgiven them of their sin and reconciled them to the Father.

Many evangelicals feel there needs to be more stress on personal conversion in the liturgical tradition. I spoke, for example,
with Dr. Richard Lovelace, professor of church history at Gordon-Conwell Theological Seminary in Wenham, Massachusetts.
Although Dr. Lovelace is a Presbyterian, his entry into Christianity was through the Episcopal church. When as a young man
Richard was searching for peace with God, he asked several
Episcopal ministers how he could be reconciled to God. "They
all seemed to totally miss the thrust of my concern," he said,
"and told me to keep a rule or have devotions, and stop being
scrupulous. None of them directed me to Christ; they assumed
that I knew Christ in a personal sense." He went on to say,
"This is a weakness in non-evangelical Protestantism . . . liturgical churches need to remake the discovery that Martin Luther
made—that the holiness and righteousness of Christ is imputed
to us. Without this Reformational sense you are left suspended
in a state of grace that is internal. You end up having to recom-
mend yourself to God instead of understanding that you rest on
the righteousness of Christ."

Evangelicals are characterized by a sense of simple gospel
trust—trust, not in themselves, not in their works, not in their
spirituality, not in their good works, but in Christ and Christ
alone for salvation. This evangelical sense that Christ saved *me,*
even *me* from sin and death is one of the major reasons why
Evangelicals in the liturgical churches are so enthused by the
liturgy. The liturgy celebrates the gospel; it glories in the work
of Christ and praises God for the mystery of salvation.

Second, evangelicals are characterized by a deep concern to
be orthodox. Although most lay evangelicals do not have a deep
grasp of theology, they have a solid commitment to what the
church has always believed. Evangelicals have a strong sense of
biblical authority; they firmly believe that God became incar-

nate in the womb of the virgin Mary; they regard Jesus as fully God and fully man; they look upon his death as a victory over sin and the power of evil and a once-for-all sacrifice for sin; they believe in a physical bodily resurrection from the dead, the ascension and the reality of the coming again of Christ to judge the living and the dead.

These two characteristics—personal faith and a deep commitment to orthodoxy, result in evangelicals being good worshipers. Since the liturgy itself re-enacts the Christ-Event and is filled with images of orthodoxy, evangelicals tend to participate in the liturgy meaningfully. The liturgy becomes a retelling and reliving of the evangelical experience and conviction. When evangelicals sing the *Gloria in Excelsis Deo,* confess their sin, listen to the Word proclaimed and preached, recite the Creed, pray the intercessory prayer, pass the Kiss of Peace, sing the *Sanctus,* proclaim the mystery, and walk forward to eat the bread and drink the wine, they do so out of experience. What the liturgy says and does the evangelical has experienced—and experiences again every time the liturgy is done. This enthusiasm and zeal for the gospel told and acted out in the liturgy assists in accomplishing what every liturgical church wants—a liturgy that rings with authenticity, a liturgy that rises above ritualism and participates in the event it represents, a liturgy that is compelling, a liturgy that is a powerful experience of the healing and comforting presence of the risen Lord.

A third characteristic of evangelicalism is a kind of Holy Writ movement. The evangelical attitude toward the Scripture is almost Jewish. The Scripture is held as the ultimate authority in all matters of faith and practice. It is read, studied, and memorized by Evangelicals. For example, the Reverend John Throop, now rector of the Church of the Mediator in Chicago, tells of his experience with the Bible in the evangelical tradition: "When I was a student I went to the Episcopal church in the morning for worship and the Bible church in the evening for Scripture study." Now, John Throop and other ministers in the liturgical tradition like him who have been influenced by the evangelical emphasis on Scripture are seeking to give scriptural preaching a more central place in their worship. Reverend Throop says, "I believe in expository preaching and careful celebration of the Eucharist . . . I think both Word and sacrament deserve equal time." While evangelicals who come into the liturgical tradition

will have a strong attachment to a eucharistic spirituality, they
will not generally lessen their commitment to biblical preaching
and Scripture studies. Evangelicals do not want book report sermons or sermons that make little or no reference to the Scripture of the day. They want to hear an exposition of the text, a
proclamation of Christ and a call to Christian duty.

Another strength of evangelicalism is its concern for evangelism and mission. Since the evangelical movement is a kind of
missionary movement within the larger church, evangelicals
have been deeply influenced by the mission mandate. This sense
of mission extends not only to evangelizing the non-churched,
but it also results in evangelicals' looking into their vocation as
a mission. The Reverend Robert McFarlane, rector of St. Barnabas Episcopal Church, says, "Evangelicals have a sense of mission. They often talk of how their future vocations can be offered to Christ. They seem to make a connection between their
religious convictions and the work in the secular world. But
Episcopalians have to be taught that idea. They tend to divide
their world between worship on the one hand and work on the
other hand, not seeing the relationship between the two."

In sum, evangelicals bring to the liturgical tradition these
strengths—the sense of personal conversion, a deep concern to
be orthodox, an attachment and love for the Scripture, and a
sense of mission. I do not intend to suggest that all liturgical
churches are lacking in these areas. Some definitely are. Others
are not. My real point is that these strengths combined with the
six drawing cards of the liturgical church mentioned in the
opening chapters (mystery, worship, sacraments, historical identity, affirmation of the ecumenical church, and a holistic spirituality) make for an unusual church in which the best of the evangelical tradition and the liturgical tradition are brought together.

Indeed, the same can be said for the evangelical churches. The
life and ministry of the local evangelical community can be
greatly enhanced by learning from the liturgical tradition and
drawing from its strengths.

Dr. Lovelace, an expert on renewal, claims that his research in
renewal demonstrates that "every awakening brought a convergence of the Catholic (liturgical) and Protestant traditions. The
most obvious example of the convergence is what I call the jus-
tification-sanctification balance."

The point is that evangelicals bring to surface the justification emphasis of the Christian faith—the need for a personal discovery that God in Jesus Christ has saved *me*. But too often the evangelical tradition stays there. It does not carry the convert further into sanctification, into growth in Christ. Here then is the contribution of the liturgical tradition. Its emphasis on growth through worship, the sacraments, spirituality and the sense of belonging to the whole community of Christ stretches the convert. One of these emphases without the other is a truncated Christianity. We need both. Consequently, evangelicals and the liturgical tradition need each other. We can no longer condemn and judge each other. We can no longer remain behind the walls of separation we have built against each other. We can no longer perpetuate the caricatures we have drawn of each other. Yes, there will be some on both sides who will continue the myths. But we must rise above them, above pettiness, above spiritual pride, and affirm the whole church of Christ and our need for each other.

Dr. Lovelace also said that his research demonstrates "that unity and renewal go hand in hand . . . maybe the two are co-inherent." All God's people want renewal. Perhaps one of the prices we will have to pay to achieve that renewal is to get rid of our prejudices against each other. Not long ago I heard Robert Schuller, a highly controversial figure among both evangelical and liturgical people say, "You know, I think in another hundred years or so people are going to look back on the period between the Reformation and the twentieth century as the second Dark Ages of the Church." My ears perked up at this statement, and I wondered why he would say that.

"I believe," he went on to say, "that the divisions which have haunted the church over the last four centuries have begun in our time to be healed. The walls that have separated us are being broken down. A great new convergence of the traditions are occurring which will change the face of the church in the next hundred years."

I hope he is right.

I think he is.

And I think the confluence between the evangelical and liturgical tradition is a sign of spiritual health, a sign of renewal in our times.

About the Contributors

ISABEL ANDERS has written for a number of religious magazines including *Christian Life, The Living Church, Christianity Today, Interlit, Quiet Hour, New Oxford Review, Innovations, Eternity,* and *Partnership.* She lives in Chicago with her husband, the Reverend John R. Throop, and their daughter, Sarah. Isabel is currently working on a book of reflections on Advent.

MICHAEL ANDERSON serves as curate at St. Gregory's Episcopal Church in Deerfield, Illinois, where he lives with his wife and three children. He graduated from the Prairie Bible Institute and from Wheaton College. He also received the M.Div. from Nashotah House, an Episcopal seminary in Nashotah, Wisconsin.

JAMES JOHNSON is currently Director of Resource Development for World Relief Corporation in Wheaton, Illinois. He is also Acquisitions Editor for Harvest House Publishers. He is founder and director of Johnson and Johnson Literary Agency and serves as adjunct professor in journalism at Wheaton College Graduate School. James graduated from Moody Bible Institute and the University of Michigan. He has authored twelve books including *How to Enjoy Life and Not Feel Guilty.*

DAVID NEFF is Associate Editor for *Christianity Today.* He graduated from Loma Linda University and received the M.Div. from Andrews University. David has also pursued additional studies at San Francisco Theological Seminary.

LAVONNE NEFF is currently a free-lance editor. She graduated from Loma Linda University and received an M.A. in Religion from Andrews University. She is the author of numerous articles and the translator of Jacques Ellul's *Money and Power.*

JOHN SKILLEN is assistant professor of English at Gordon College. He graduated from Gordon College and received an M.A. and a Ph.D. from Duke University, where he was a James B. Duke Fellow and a John L. Livesay Instructor in English.

ROBERT WEBBER, Th.D., is professor of theology at Wheaton College. In addition to conducting "Worship Is a Verb" workshops in various cities throughout the United States, Webber has authored a number of articles and books on the subject. His most recent writings include: *Common Roots: A Call to Evangelical Maturity*, *Secular Humanism: Threat and Challenge*, *Worship Old and New*, and *Worship Is a Verb*.